Moving to IRELAND

A Guide to Living and Investing

Brendan Connolly & Peter Steadman

COMPENDIUM

Compendium Publishing Ltd
5 Gerrard Street
London W1V 7LJ

© Brendan Connolly and Peter steadman

A CIP record for this book is available from
the British Library

ISBN 1 85915 150 7

Contents

Foreword

by

ANDY ROGERS
ASSISTANT GENERAL MANAGER
BANK OF IRELAND

For many centuries, people have moved over and back across the Irish Sea — seeking work and setting up businesses. Some moved permanently, others temporarily.

In the early 1950s, those moving to Britain far outnumbered those returning, while by the end of the 1990s this has completely reversed — for example, in 1997 Ireland's population grew by a net 15,000 returnees.

Ireland, of course, has gone through a total economic transformation over that period. The strong growth pattern of recent years continues, and real GNP growth for 1998 will be 9 percent. Recent changes to Ireland's Corporate Tax regime will continue to boost inward investment and economic growth well into the next century.

Bank of Ireland, founded in 1783, has a widespread network throughout these islands. Over the past 200 years, the Bank has been a major participant in the evolution of the Irish economy. In Britain and Ireland over 13,000 staff and 500 branches provide the most comprehensive range of services to customers.

Our staff in any Bank of Ireland branch, whether in Britain or Ireland, are available to assist business and personal customers with their financial needs. Just call us.

We are pleased to have supported Brendon Connolly and Peter Steadman as they prepared *Moving to Ireland: A Guide to Living and Investing*. Whether you are thinking of moving or have decided to do so, or are just interested in understanding how Ireland functions — *Moving to Ireland* has all the essential details.

I know you will find this book a most useful source.

Introduction

What kind of people decide to make that dramatic change of a lifetime, to up sticks and move abroad, specifically to the Republic of Ireland? New-Agers seeking a gentler, nature-centred existence untroubled by the authorities? Incurable romantics drawn to a country of which they may have only the fuzziest knowledge? Good-Lifers tending their goats on a remote small-holding?

Nature-centred, fuzzy-notioned, romantic — yes, all of these take the plunge. But it's not just the eccentric that make the move: you, too, could be the ideal candidate. Ireland almost certainly has something to offer everyone, if only they stop to consider the possibilities and choices available!

In the past 10 to 15 years, powered especially by its membership of the European Union which it joined in 1973, Ireland has grown from Celtic Fringe to Celtic Tiger. Along with the influx of industrial, commercial and infrastructure investment and the radically growing and changing economy thus generated, have come major changes of social outlook. New Irish laws concerning divorce, separation, domestic violence, homosexuality, child welfare and employment equality all bear witness to a major philosophical change and national confidence — and all of this has been accomplished without losing that essential Irishness, the 'craic', the family and community values and love of place that have been long associated with Ireland and its people

Tens of thousands of people from the UK, as the table below shows, from perfectly average backgrounds, have moved to the Republic of Ireland for the better social welfare benefits, leisure facilities and lifestyle. Business people, often initially on short-term tours of duty to help start up new commercial and industrial businesses fuelled by inward investment, decide to settle permanently and take advantage of the quality of life and the educational opportunities. The Irish themselves are returning to a home that now has such positive things to offer — most importantly and crucially, the employment opportunities that did not exist in the talent-exporting days when they first left to work abroad. High-flyers who work in the UK and Europe during the week now commute to Ireland for the weekends or buy properties there as investments as well as homes.

If you are looking for a second or holiday home, Ireland's the place. If you want to invest in or start up a business of your own — take advantage of the many grants and facilities being made available. Even football clubs have thought about it, both England's Wimbledon and Scotland's Clydebank have considered moves to Dublin. Ireland is the sort of place that people of every circumstance can seriously and sensibly consider as a home. With its own unique and special ways, Ireland can be as attractive a place to move to and live in as more popular destinations such as Spain and France or more traditional countries such as Australia, New Zealand, Canada and the United States of America.

This book will give you a flavour of the country and its people, the essential services such as health and education, transport and communications, the taxation, mortgage, financial and legal hurdles that must be cleared in order to help ensure a smooth and successful transition to Ireland. You will need it, particularly if you live in Britain — for all of Ireland's centuries of close contact with the United Kingdom and use of the English language, it has remained a different and individual country. It is as foreign, as sovereign and as proud of its nationhood as any other.

Though not directly impinging on the Republic of Ireland, the 'Troubles', as they are known, and the associated violence of Northern Ireland have certainly coloured people's attitudes to the island as a whole. The Republic of Ireland has suffered from this poor opinion, especially among the English. It is, therefore, enormously gratifying to see the real progress being made as the conflicting parties begin their slow and painful climb from confrontation to a political *modus vivendi*; a real chance now exists, the first for a generation, for a softening of the rigid attitudes held so long by all parties.

A lasting reconciliation and acceptance of each other's cultural history wil take years to develop, just as the antipathy itself has lasted for centuries — but the rewards are almost beyond measure, for Northern Ireland more in terms of societal well-being than pure economics, and for the Republic in the increase in confidence, security and cross-border commercial opportunities it will bring.

As for the immediate purpose of this book, there are tourist guides and histories aplenty, just look at the travel and history sections of any half-decent bookshop: but these will not provide the technical answers to the complicated questions that you should be considering. No, what you need is a manual or 'how-to' guide with a good directory of useful contacts and addresses — and that is precisely the purpose of this book; a comprehensive overview of the many questions you should be asking about conditions and practices in the Republic of Ireland.

This book is not a traditional 'tourist taster', but rather examines in a systematic way the whole process of making such a major life-change, looking in some detail at each stage of the process, suggesting many of the things to which you should give serious thought and consideration, and presenting some helpful solutions and places to go for further information. This book aims to organise your thoughts and identify your key requirements as well as provide substantive solutions.

One point to note: it is worth mentioning at an early stage that this book does not cover the six counties of Northern Ireland, partly because the North's legal and financial systems as a part of the United Kingdom are generally similar to those of the British mainland, and partly because describing two dissimilar systems in one book would be confusing to author and reader alike.

GOVERNANCE

Before we begin the book proper it is appropriate to take just a few moments to describe the constitutional framework and governance of the state.

The Republic of Ireland is a sovereign, independent, democratic state whose current constitution was adopted by plebiscite in 1937. It is divided into four provinces of historic antiquity and includes 26 of the 32 counties into which the island of Ireland has been traditionally divided for many centuries:

Provinces	Counties
Connacht	Galway, Leitrim, Mayo, Roscommon, Sligo.
Leinster	Carlow, Dublin, Kildare, Kilkenny, Laoighis, Longford, Louth, Meath, Offaly, Westmeath, Wexford, Wicklow.
Munster	Clare, Cork, Kerry, Limerick, Tipperary, Waterford.
Ulster	South — Cavan, Donegal, Monaghan. North — Antrim, Armagh, Down, Fermanagh, Londonderry and Tyrone.

Very roughly, Connacht lies to the west and north-west, Leinster to the east, Munster to the south and south-west and Ulster to the north and north-east.

The Irish constitution allows for a head of state, the President (*Uachtaran-na-hEireann*), who is elected by direct vote of the people for a period of seven years. In common with many written constitutions, power is then divided between the three branches of government:

- THE LEGISLATURE (*Oireachtas*) consists of the President and two Houses, a House of Representatives (*Dail Eireann*) and a Senate (*Seanad Eireann*). The Dail is elected by the people using a system of proportional representation, whilst the Senate is part appointed and part elected indirectly from various panels of candidates. The main parties represented in the Dail are Fianna Fail, Fine Gael and Labour (not connected with the United Kingdom Labour Party).

- THE EXECUTIVE is drawn from the Dail and must have the confidence of that chamber. It is headed by the Prime Minister (*Taoiseach*) and the Deputy Prime Minister (*Tanaiste*) and a cabinet of Ministers.

- THE JUDICIARY is independent and consists of Courts of First Instance. It includes the High Court (*Ard Chuirt*), the courts of local and limited jurisdiction and a Court of Final Appeal (*Cuirt Uachtarach*).

OTHER ESSENTIALS

- Ireland's capital is the City of Dublin
- The official languages are Irish (the national language) and English (the principal vehicle for most communication)
- The national flag is the tricolour of green, white and orange, which represents peaceful coexistence between the two politico-religious traditions within the island
- The currency is the Punt or Irish Pound of 100 Pence (soon to be replaced by the Euro); and, finally,
- Ireland uses the metric system for weights and measures.

CHAPTER 1

Why Ireland?

Leprechauns, fairies and the little people; Guinness, the Emerald Isle of rolling, empty countryside and traffic-free lanes; Guinness and friendly people, warm welcomes, pubs, harps, poteen and, oh, did we mention Guinness?

Such are the classical, clichéed images conjured by the name 'Ireland', to which we can add those modern icons of *Riverdance*, golf, the Irish lottery and Bob Geldof's designer stubble. It's certainly easy to be lyrical about the Republic, particularly after seeing it, lush, green and friendly, during a languid summer holiday one of the increasingly popular short off season breaks or as part of a trip to Landsdowne Road for the annual Five Nations rugby football match. But this is to sell Ireland a long way short — though within every stereotype there does indeed lurk a truism — and these seem to us to be as fine and enjoyable a set of truths as you could wish for (unless you do actually see any little green folk, in which case you should probably stop drinking and/or contact one of the more lurid, tabloid newspapers!).

What of the Emerald Isle of rolling, empty countryside and traffic-free lanes? The geographical charms of Ireland have been extolled and appreciated down the years. A small country of about 69,000 sq km (26,600 sq miles) of land and 1,400 sq km (530 sq miles) of inland water, Ireland is, nonetheless, home to a wide variety of scenery and landscapes.

The Gulf Stream exercises a benign influence keeping the island wonderfully temperate and allowing a wide range of plants to thrive. Ireland's 3,200km (2,000 miles) of coastline ensure that no point is more than 115km (70 miles) or so from the sea. Examples of typical temperatures are:

Period	Months	Temperatures
Coldest	January, February,	4-7°C (39-45°F)
Warmest	July, August	14-16°C (57-61°F) but can reach 25°C (77°F)
Sunniest	May, June,	5-7 hours of sunshine a day

Of course, Ireland is also renowned for its legendary rainfall, as a Kerry saying has it: 'if you can see Valencia Island then it'll soon be raining, if you can't, then it already is.' The average annual rainfall ranges from about 760mm (30in) in the east to twice that amount in the west, as the rain-laden clouds come sailing out of the Atlantic to meet the Irish landmass and unload themselves. It is not the quantity so much as the frequency that has led to those poetic effusions over 'emerald isles', the softness of the panorama through a fine mist, the shiny wetness glinting off the landscape, the almost spiritual glory as shafts of damp sunlight break through the clouds, dancing across and illuminating the chequerboard of a frequently empty-seeming countryside.

The geological heart of Ireland is formed by a rolling limestone plain that ranges in height from 60-120m (200-400ft) above sea level with occasional undulations, rising to 300m (1,000ft.) Rich, well watered pastures such as Tipperary's Golden Vale and the Bluegrass country of Kildare occupy this land along with the extensive peat bogs of Offaly.

Contrasting with the gentle inland areas are the remarkably rugged and mountainous coasts, though only about 15 percent of the island actually rises higher than 213m (700ft) above sea level. The far south-west county of Kerry boasts Ireland's highest peak at 1,041m (3,414ft.) The south-east contains the oddly isolated Wicklow Mountains, whilst the whole western side beyond the River Shannon is noted for its much loved though austere scenery stretching from Donegal through Sligo, Mayo, Galway and Clare.

With an estimated population of just 3,661,000 people in 1997 and 57 percent of those living in urban areas, Ireland is remarkably empty and this only adds to the present day attractiveness of the country with its expansive, unspoilt countryside, uncluttered vistas and sense of peace and quiet.

As well as its geographical charms, the Ireland we enjoy today is but the sum of its historical past and there is no shortage of that! In a sense, Ireland's recorded history starts with an invasion and in many ways invasion becomes a constant companion to the Irish psyche. The first, mythical invasion was that recounted in the ancient *Leabar Gabala*, or *Book of Invasions*: the arrival of Heremon, Hiber and Ir, the three sons of Mileadh of Spain supposedly around the time of Alexander the Great. Then came the Celts, who arrived in the fourth century BC from mainland Europe, interestingly not via Britain. The Celts ruled Ireland at the time when Christianity arrived with St. Patrick in 432AD, and were still there when the Norsemen invaded. They founded such cities as Dublin, Cork and Limerick and were followed closely by the Anglo-Normans, who first set foot in Bannow Bay in County Wexford in 1169AD, a landing that heralded seven and a half centuries of successively Norman, English, then British, involvement. This cultural mix has had a big impact on the culture of Ireland.

To misquote a famous saying, after centuries of peace Switzerland invented the cuckoo clock, but the centuries of conflict in Ireland have been accompanied by an extraordinary level of learning and artistic excellence, especially of the written and spoken word. There is the *Leabar Gabala* already mentioned, the *Tain Bo Cualgne*, a pagan epic from around the time of Christ, the extant portions of the *Psalter of Cashel* and the magnificent *Book of Kells* on display in Dublin: all bear witness to a love of myth and respect for the power of words in both spoken and written forms.

The flowering of Christianity had an enormous influence on mainland Britain as well as on a wider Europe, as Irish missionaries took their learning and faith back to the Continent right up to the time of the Norman invasions, through such figures as Columba in Iona, Cataldus of Taranto, Killian of Franconia, Colman of Lower Austria and the Irish monasteries founded in Peronne on the Marne, Cologne, Ratisbon, Vienna and many others.

Moving across the centuries, once the English state had become politically dominant, so the English language effectively ousted Irish Gaelic. Far from destroying Irish culture, however, there has been a flowering of Anglo-Irish writing that continues to this day with such authors and playwrights as Oliver Goldsmith, Jonathan Swift,

Richard Brinsley Sheridan, Oscar Wilde, William Butler Yeats, James Joyce, John Millington Synge, Sean O'Casey, George Bernard Shaw, Samuel Beckett, Bram Stoker, Brendan Behan, Brian Friel, Sebastian Barry and many, many more.

Music, too, has always played a vital part in life (and death — the Irish wake is another legendary event), originally as part of the minstrel-cum-bardic tradition of story-telling. During festivals and social events the story-telling was accompanied by harp, bagpipe, bodhran drum, whistle and fiddle, and dancing, another great Irish tradition. In modern times, Irish music has been a significant part of the global popular music scene embracing The Chieftains, James Galway, U2, Boyzone, Van Morrison, Thin Lizzy, Boomtown Rats, Moving Hearts, Clannad, Sinhead O'Connor, The Cranberries and a plethora of other individuals, groups and bands covering every type of music from traditional Irish through classical orchestral works to rock and punk.

Architecturally Ireland is very rich, with archaeological sites stretching back to the Neolithic and Iron Ages, and many ruins of religious buildings, castles and forts. Not every site is ruined: there are many beautiful houses and gardens extant ranging from fine town houses and elegant small country homes, to the magnificence of large, landed estates with their parks and formal gardens.

Dublin — that recently celebrated its 1,000th birthday — is often said to be the finest Georgian city in the world. It contains a wealth of splendid buildings. Despite some losses in recent years, the city still maintains an impressive endowment of buildings of architectural, historic, aesthetic or cultural distinction. Maintaining (or in some cases restoring) their vitality is a key element in positioning Dublin as a European capital of note. While quality of life is a vital ingredient for attracting and attaching people of talent and innovation, high levels of enterprise need high quality environments: these two factors are inextricably linked in modern economies. It is also the case that the fulfilment of Dublin's aspirations to become one of Europe's leading tourist destinations depends on its success in maintaining its built heritage.

Still extant gems include Trinity College, the Bank of Ireland (that until 1803 housed Ireland's own Parliament), Merrion Square, Leinster House, Fitzwilliam Street, Iveagh House and many more buildings, streets and churches. One is certainly struck by the lack of modern high-rise buildings, the prevalent characteristic of the skyline of a modern city. Extensive renovation work on some of the important buildings has been, or is being, undertaken. Ireland now has a Heritage Council with statutory responsibility for conservation and restoration. Recent years have also seen the construction of a significant amount of contemporary architecture of good quality, such as the Civic Offices, Temple Bar and the International Financial Services Centre. But remember, Dublin is not the whole of Ireland and many cities and towns have their own architectural gems that are equally worth visiting.

Finally, as well as the countryside and history of Ireland, there's the genealogy. There is a good chance that you yourself are at least part Irish! One of the major reasons for Ireland's uncluttered landscape is the fact that the Industrial Revolution passed it by, and the agrarian lifestyle could not support a population that reached one-seventh of the entire British Isles. Over the past four centuries, and especially since the Great Famine of the mid-1840s, literally millions of Irish have emigrated to the four corners of the globe and as a result are well represented in all the English-speaking nations. Maybe you have an Irish surname, a tradition of Irish forenames or perhaps a family story that claims to give you Irish blood coursing through your veins! Genealogy and ancestor tracing is a very important way for many people to explore their roots, real or imagined - witness America's President Reagan visiting his 'family home'.

Today there is now a flourishing industry devoted to mining the rich seams of records so painstakingly collected over centuries by church, state and private archive, and it can be a fascinating process to embark upon, albeit one that needs time and dedication more than money. Who knows, you may even trace some living relatives! There are a host of commercial and do-it-yourself organisations with the resources and know-how to help you assemble your own family tree and a good starting point is a leaflet published by the Bord Failte (Irish Tourist Board) that explains the process and gives a comprehensive list of contacts should you wish to pursue things in earnest.

CHAPTER 2

The Benefits of Moving to Ireland

The last chapter looked at the first impressions of Ireland — beautiful landscape, good food and drink, a fascinating history, a cultural heritage that stands comparison with any in the world — but few people can make a sensible life-change on a whim: there are other, less romantic reasons to move to Ireland; let's review some of them.

YOU ARE NOT ALONE

People are retiring much earlier these days and it is not unusual to meet someone who intends to retire, or who already has retired, at 50. While many people look forward to their 'third' age with the anticipation of an end to a long working life, retiring early requires some form of occupation. As a result of all that it has to offer the active retiree, Ireland has become a hugely popular destination for people to retire to over the last ten years. According to a study by the Institute of Irish Studies at the University of Liverpool, the number of UK State Pensions and Widow's Benefits paid to recipients living in the Irish Republic has grown from almost 40,000 in 1984 to over 74,000 in 1995 as people have seen the benefits of retiring across the Irish Sea.

Despite 100 years of net emigration, recent records point to a gathering trend for people to return to the country of their birth. According to the Department of Enterprise and Employment, involuntary emigration, as the Irish call their export of economically-active people seeking work abroad, has fallen sharply, indeed reversed, from its post-war peak outflow of 43,900 in 1988/89 to a net inflow of 8,000 in 1995/96 and 15,000 in 1996/97; a sure sign of a buoyant economy and the rise in good employment opportunities being created at home.

The information on the following table is drawn from the Irish Central Statistics Office Statistical Release October 1997, *Population and Migration Estimates.*

IMMIGRANTS TO THE REPUBLIC OF IRELAND IN 000s

YEAR	1992	1993	1994	1995	1996	1997
(Ending April)						
Total Immigration	40.7	34.8	30.1	31.2	39.2	44.0
Split by Origination						
From UK	22.7	17.5	15.2	15.6	17.6	20.0
Rest of EU	6.5	6.6	5.8	6.3	7.2	8.1
USA	4.6	5.0	4.3	3.8	6.4	6.6
Rest of World	6.9	5.7	4.8	5.5	8.0	9.3
Split by Gender						
Male	21.8	17.5	14.8	14.7	18.8	21.6
Female	18.9	17.3	15.3	16.6	20.4	22.4
Split by Age						
0-14	6.2	5.6	4.4	5.3	6.6	6.4
15-24	12.5	10.3	9.7	8.0	10.9	13.8
25-44	16.5	14.5	12.0	14.6	16.9	18.1
45-64	4.1	3.6	3.1	2.6	3.6	4.4
65+	1.4	0.8	0.9	0.7	1.2	1.3
Net Emigration	0.4	4.7	1.9			
Net Immigration	7.4				8.0	15.0

So it is not just the young and skilled who previously had to live abroad to pursue a career that matched their education and aspirations, but older people too, moving to a country that can now offer the levels of social welfare and health treatment that become more important as we gain in age. The social and moral impact of this change and the boost to national self-confidence is almost impossible to measure quantitavely, yet is tangible to any visitor.

As for tourism, Ireland welcomed 4,739,000 visitors in 1996, a remarkable 51 percent increase since 1992! You can drawn your own conclusions from that, but we think that it is safe to say that many more people are discovering the delights and beauty of Ireland and further on in this book we will be mentioning some of these in greater detail. Our best advice, given that 4.7 million people cannot be wrong, is to hurry up and be one of them!

RETIREMENT BENEFITS

Many people suppose that when they retire life stops and they are doomed to stay at home, vegetate and lose interest in the wider world. This could not be further from the truth. The vast majority of people now look forward to retirement as a time for travel, a time to pursue long postponed special interests, to take up new activities, face new challenges and, in the case of Ireland, move to a country that still has a strong sense of community. They can often top up their existing pensions (Irish state pensions are typically more generous than those in the United Kingdom) and take advantage of many extra perks, benefits and concessions.

The life style is, in most cases, quite comfortable and the pace of life, especially outside the major conurbations, is very much the same as decades ago. The crime rate is still comparatively low which is an extremely important consideration and people do generally feel quite safe.

The common views amongst people who have retired to Ireland is one of satisfaction with a decision well made and of belonging to a recognisable community. With travel times to the British mainland cities being no more than two hours by air and with easy ferry travel — which is slower, but cheap and getting cheaper — you are less likely to suffer the sense of isolation or of having abandoned your loved ones and friends.— And the language is the same (almost!)

As has been suggested earlier, there are several perks available to those who retire to the Republic and we have listed the most significant ones below. Remember, however, that the state retirement age is not the same for all countries, for example in the United Kingdom the current retirement age for men is 65 and for women 60. A woman who is entitled to a retirement pension in both the UK and Ireland may get their UK state pension at 60, but will have to wait until 65 to receive her Irish one.

As a modern democracy Ireland has gradually built an increasingly complex social security net and just some of the benefits that can apply to the elderly are:

- Old age/retirement pensions
- Aged 80 allowance
- Living alone allowance
- Pre-retirement allowance
- Early farm retirement scheme
- Widows and widowers benefits
- Invalidity benefits
- Disability allowance
- Blind pension and welfare allowance
- Mobility allowance
- Carer's allowance
- Death grant

The main perks are:

- Free travel on road and rail (countrywide)
- Free electricity
- Free bottled gas allowance
- Free natural gas allowance
- Free colour television licence
- Free telephone rental
- Fuel scheme

So, Ireland is a land of milk and honey for the retired? Well, not exactly. Many of these benefits and allowances are means-tested. Having been a relatively poor country for so long Ireland has had to be very careful about how it allocated its limited resources between the various services of a modern state — health, education, welfare being foremost amongst the big spenders. Thus it is that the welfare system has grown gradually with benefits targeted at those in the greatest financial need. There is a second form of allocation, not based on your means but on your history of contributions to the Pay Related Social Insurance system. This is a government run, compulsory, contributory, social security and welfare scheme that is designed to award payments to eligible recipients based on the level of their 'fund'; no contributions, no benefits.

The rules, therefore, for obtaining these benefits can be complex and the qualifications will vary from benefit to benefit. Your capital resources as well as your income will be added to the equation — though not the value of your own home if you live in it — however if you give away or otherwise distribute your capital this, too, may well be added back for the purposes of assessing your eligibility to claim. For older people, (those over 66) it is possible to sell your house and still keep up to £75,000 of the capital thus raised, outside the means testing formula so long as the proceeds are used to fund alternative rented accommodation or to meet the fees of a registered nursing home.

Some benefits are administered by the central government's social welfare system and others by the Regional Health Boards. They have differing methodologies of assessing someone's means, so that meeting the requirements to qualify for one benefit does not automatically make you eligible for another.

Without causing undue alarm, hopefully, you now realise that although there are a wide range of benefits and allowances on offer it is by no means a simple task to obtain them, and that the circumstances of each individual claimant must be assessed. Application forms are generally available from Post Offices, Regional Health Board offices and Citizens Information Centres. As a consequence you will almost certainly require some help and guidance on the ground and a good first port of call would be the local Citizens Information Centre where free, confidential advice is available.

Under EU legislation the payments that you have made into your own national social security system can be aggregated with your Irish ones and it is on the basis of the combined history that claimants can be assessed for certain benefits, so have as much documentary evidence of your payment history as possible by applying to your national social security system and, once in Ireland, to:

EU Section Pension Services Office
College Road
Sligo
Tel: (01) 874 8444 or (071) 69800

Ireland also has bilateral arrangements with a number of non-European Union countries regarding social security, these being

Canada, Australia, the USA, Quebec and New Zealand and covers the operation of the following benefits:

- Old age / retirement pensions
- Widows and widowers benefits (called Survivors Benefits in some countries)
- Orphans benefits
- Invalidity benefits
- Death grant (not New Zealand)

If you have queries (and you almost certainly will!) concerning the portability of your social security contributions whether you come from within the European Union or outside then you should contact:

Department of Social Welfare
EU/International Section
Aras Mhic Dhiarmada
Store Street
Dublin 1
Tel: (01) 874 8444

As well as these perks, a number of establishments offer special reductions to pensioners. These concessions are granted purely at the discretion of the firms involved and can be changed or even withdrawn at short notice. In general they may be available at cinemas, theatres, race meetings, zoos, the Royal Dublin Show, Croke Park and other Gaelic Athletic Association grounds, greyhound racing, the National Concert Hall, dry cleaners, hairdressers and some cable link companies and DIY stores. Golden Holidays for people aged 60 or more are available at a number of holiday resorts and all Dublin municipal swimming pools grant free admission during public sessions.

There are a number of travel concessions. B&I and Sealink Ferries give reductions on sea travel between Britain and Ireland to holders of a Free Travel Pass. Under the Rail Europe scheme people aged 60 and over may receive reductions of between 30 percent and 50 percent of the standard fares charged by railway and shipping companies in nearly all European countries. Airlines also offer a range of reductions on most fares between Britain and Ireland, too.

You should check with your local council for details of the concessions particular to your chosen area. A good source of impartial, independent information on these, and other matters are the nationwide network of over 80 Citizens Information Centres. They make no charge for their services and can provide advice on topics such as social welfare, health services, redundancy, income tax, housing, family law, consumer affairs and local organisations and services as well as assisting with form filling, appealing against decisions and other compliance procedures beloved of bureaucracies the world over.

QUALITY OF LIFE

English is the common language (except in the Gaeltacht Irish speaking areas) which means that the most important and frustrating barrier to life in another culture and country does not exist. So that even though Ireland is a thoroughly individual country, quite different from Britain in so many ways, with its own unique culture, day-to-day communication is not a problem. The nice thing is how familiar yet curiously different so many things will seem, whether an accent, a food product with local packaging, road signs, social interaction, radio stations or driving through a small town with its brightly coloured shops and pubs and the very Irish signs hanging from walls and doorways with their characteristic style and history.

The Irish attitude is one that always seems relaxed, happy-go-lucky, always has time for a chat and does not seem to set great store by punctuality. You are not moving to a totally alien land, just somewhere interestingly different and the best way to enjoy your new adventure is to join in and be part of your new, local community. Ask neighbours around for lunch or tea (a drop of whiskey might be even better!). Chat to people in the shops, the bank or Post Office. It is the same anywhere, if your attitude is positive and you make the effort to embrace, to get involved, to really live your new life and surroundings then people will warm to you in return.

On the other hand it does no harm to maintain contact with your fellow countrymen through an expatriate club, but not to the extent of relying solely on this for your social and mental support, otherwise you can so easily miss out on the reasons you moved here in the first place.

The sense of community is strong in Ireland and the family is still the central, social unit. The quality of life is particularly good for families, especially the freedom that children can still enjoy in comparative safety. Children of all ages are to be seen playing, cycling, walking and generally socialising without the need for constant parental supervision. In the rural areas the seemingly endless and almost traffic-free roads, farms, forests and beaches offer a wealth of freedom and choice for a healthy childhood.

DUBLIN

As Ireland's capital and largest city Dublin is worthy of particular note as it is more than likely that you will want to visit the city and its facilities from time to time; in truth you would be missing out on one of Ireland's greatest assets if you never get there.

We have already mentioned the unique, architectural splendour of Dublin with its magnificent Georgian buildings, low-level skyline and wide central avenues, but one can add to that its pedestrianised zones, choice of shops and retail outlets, its museums and galleries, educational facilities, its cinemas, theatres and concert halls, its sports stadia, clubs, pubs, restaurants and nightlife plus its good public transport infrastructure so that you can easily get to them all.

For information on things to see and do in Dublin you should contact:

Dublin Tourism Centre
Suffolk Street
Dublin 2
Tel: (01) 605 7797 *for enquiries only from the United Kingdom*

Dublin is also a good place for business with its modern telecommunications, international airport, hotels and business centres. Furthermore in 1997 Dublin was named as Europe's top business city by *Fortune* magazine when it was awarded the 'Most Improved City for Business'. Some of the top ten cities are reviewed at right.

Dublin Airport

The planned extensions to Dublin International Airport will only enhance the attractiveness of Dublin as a centre for business and leisure. For the ten years up to 1985, passenger numbers through Dublin Airport remained stable at 2.5 million. In 1986, following the introduction of competitive fares, (primarily to the UK) numbers grew to 2.9m. A new era of aviation was heralded by Ryanair's arrival and the start of liberalisation of air transport within the EU. Following a temporary lull in 1991, as a result of the Gulf War, Dublin's passengers grew to over 9m in 1996. This growth has been generated by:

- Strong performance of the Irish economy
- Positive growth in source markets
- More competitive fares available in all markets
- Introduction of competition on existing routes
- Strong recovery by the airline industry, particularly Aer Lingus

Dublin airport boasts the strongest route-network of any airport into the UK. All five London airports are served comprehensively with over 85 flights per day. This market exceeded the 3m passenger level

COMPARING CITIES: DUBLIN AND EUROPE

FACTOR	Dublin	Amsterdam	Barcelona	Milan	London	Rome
Population (000s)	911	1,109	2,819	4,251	7,335	2,931
National unemployment rate	12%	6.6%	21.9%	12%	7.6%	12%
Manufacturing wages	$13.79	$23.01	$12.49	$17.40	$13.63	$17.40
Cities reached by air	40	133	66	53	172	77
Class A office rental (US$/sq ft)	27.02	25.87	19.66	28.78	53.88	28.78
Inflation rate	1.8%	1.7%	3.6%	4.2%	2.6%	4.2%
Cost of living index ($ to $$$$$)	$$	$$	$$	$$	$$$	$$
Violent crime rate (per 100,000)	77.5	129.4	261.2	93.6	96.4	93.6
CO2 emissions (tons per person)	9.2	9.2	5.6	7.0	10.0	7.0

last year, and is likely to become the business scheduled international route in Europe this year. Additionally, 18 United Kingdom provincial airports are also served.

Dublin airport also offers 25 European, and five United States scheduled destinations. Overall, 58 destinations are served on a scheduled basis from Dublin airport, which has 23 scheduled airlines using it.

Dublin Airport Facts and Figures:
- More than 10m passengers handled in 1997
- Biggest economic unit in Ireland
- An economic zone which accounts for about 2.1% of GNP
- The place of employment for about 9,000 people directly, and the source of another 35,000 jobs indirectly
- Used by 90 percent of the top 1000 Irish companies
- One of the fastest growing of its size
- Home to about 110 separate businesses

PRICES, INFLATION AND INTEREST RATES

It is now recognised by most people that in reality the best environment in which to live is one with low inflation, steady economic growth and moderate interest rates. Many of us have experienced periods of high inflation and interest rates and for a short period this seems just fine, our assets appear to increase in value, our borrowings diminish in value in real terms as our incomes romp ahead and we apparently earn spectacular returns on our cash balances. But we have come to realise this quickly turns sour, as prices spiral away out of reach, the real buying power of our savings is eroded and the bubble bursts with a vengeance in the classic boom-and-bust cycle so beloved (if their past performance is any guide) by British politicians.

Ireland seems largely to have squared the circle with considerable success and has managed a period of strong economic growth with historically low inflation. Interest rates have been quite high and the only major blip has been the house price boom. The real numbers are worth a quick look and the data quoted in the following paragraphs are taken from the Irish Central Statistics Office Economic Series January 1998 publication.

The best measurement of inflation and one that we are probably most familiar with is the Consumer Price Index. Most countries produce the CPI on a monthly basis as an attempt to measure the changing prices of a representative 'basket' of domestic purchases including food, clothing, housing, energy, transport, entertainment, etc.

In the case of Ireland, taking mid-November 1997 as 100, the Consumer Price All Items Index has moved from 90.9 in January 1990 to 101.9 in December 1997. This may seem a bit nebulous, but gives an average, annual inflation rate of 1.4 percent over these eight years. Looking at 1997 in isolation the Index grew by 1.9 percent.

Central Bank short-term interest rates are the driving force behind the commercially available rates that you and I have to pay (though this will change with the adoption of the Euro as Ireland's currency from the 1st of January, 1999 and the setting of European Union wide interest rates by the new Central Bank in Frankfurt.) A representative sample of Central Bank short-term and Building Societies' mortgage loan rates shows a mixed pattern, but one that is generally on the decline:

Year end	Bank Rate	Mortgage Rate
1991	10.75%	11.45%
1992	13.75%	13.99%
1993	7.00%	7.99%
1994	6.25%	7.00%
1995	6.50%	7.10%
1996	6.25%	6.75%
1997	6.75%	7.40%

Within the static nature of a book it is essentially impossible to give precise information on something as volatile and mobile as house prices, with all the unpredictable influences of economic growth, interest rates, exchange rates (if buying with a non-Punt denominated mortgage or loan), local development, fashion and any number of other factors that each work their magic.

One can, however, look at trends and suffice to say that the trend has been up (though remember, past performance is no guarantee of future outcomes!) In the more fashionable parts of Dublin it is reported that house prices are increasing by as much as 1 percent per week. This is exceptional, as Dublin is prone to the greater forces that being a capital city and principal business centre bring in their wake, but all across Ireland there has been a major surge in property costs seeing an average 20 percent increase in both 1996 and 1997 and no easing off in 1998. For greater detail on house prices and their recent movement see Chapter 9 on House Buying.

Along with the price boom there has also been something of a building boom going on, with annual dwelling completions growing by 50 percent in five years to 33,725 in 1996, 89 percent of these in the private sector.

As noted earlier, the annual rate of inflation in Ireland has been quite modest over recent years and is still below 2 percent, and has recently been nearer to those common amongst the economies of the major mainland European countries than the United Kingdom. The government is predicting an average inflation rate of 2.1 percent per annum over the next three years.

This is all the more remarkable given the rate of growth of the Irish economy — which is predicted to be 4.75 percent per annum — especially when we bear in mind the United Kingdom's historic never-ending struggle with combining sustained economic growth with low inflation.

To demonstrate the growth in the Irish economy we can look at a variety of indicators (taken from Central Statistics Office, Ireland: Economic Series, January 1998) since they all bear out the same story of rapid growth:

Indicator	1991	1996	Change
Population in 000s	3,526	3,626	+2.8%
People in work in 000s	1,134	1,297	+14.3%
People unemployed in 000s	209	191	-8.7%
Gross National Product (£m)	25,427	36,983	+45.4%
GNP per Capita (£)	7,211	10,213	+41.6%

Indicator	Jan 1992	Oct 1997	Change
Industrial Production Index 1985 base = 100	153	305	+99.3%
Imports (£m)	1,068	2,420	+126.5%
Exports (£m)	1,295	3,150	+143.2%

Even allowing for some modest price and cost inflation these remain impressive figures.

Certainly interest rates have been a key element of inflationary control and have been at rates more familiar to the British than mainland Europeans — that is higher!

Indicator	Jan 1992	Dec 1997	Change
Central Bank Short Term Facility (% pa)	10.75	6.75	-37.3%
Building Societies Mortgage Loans (% pa)	11.45	7.40	-35.4%

COST OF LIVING

As a very rough guide to help you visualise in everyday terms some of the costs of living in Ireland here are a few everyday shopping-trolley products with some typical prices, though as with any country many goods are subject to seasonal variation and you can often find cheaper and certainly more expensive:

Item	Unit	Price in Punts
Washing up liquid	1 litre	1.65
Washing powder	large	1.90
Sliced loaf	large	0.94
Chicken	medium	3.99
Potatoes	2.5 kilos	1.30
Milk	1 litre	0.70
Sugar	1 kilo	0.85
Cheddar Cheese	500gm	2.93
Margarine	400gm	0.90
Butter	227gm	0.60
Sirloin Steak	1kg	9.87
Cooking Oil	1 litre	0.61
Eggs	dozen	1.65
Coffee	100gm	2.85
Tea Bags	80 number	1.40
Cigarettes	20 number	2.88

Item	Unit	Price in Punts
Petrol	1 litre	0.61
Cheaper wine	bottle	4.99
Guinness served in a pub	pint	2.05
Lager served in a pub	pint	2.25

CRIME

The 11,600 or so men and women of the *Garda Siochana*, or Police Force, are responsible for the maintenance of law and order within the Republic. The Garda's own publication, *Corporate Strategy Policy Document 1993-1997*, though not recommended for light reading, does provide some useful, official statistics that support the generally held perception that crime is less common in Ireland than in other European countries.

With the essential caveats that Ireland suffers like other countries from a feeling that violence within society is becoming more

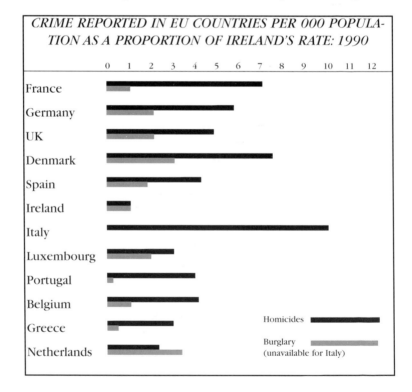

CRIME REPORTED IN EU COUNTRIES PER 000 POPULATION AS A PROPORTION OF IRELAND'S RATE: 1990

common, that crime has shown an increase over the past 30 years and that comparing international statistics is difficult due to the different legal systems, definitions and data collection methodologies in use, the graphs in this section well illustrate the point.

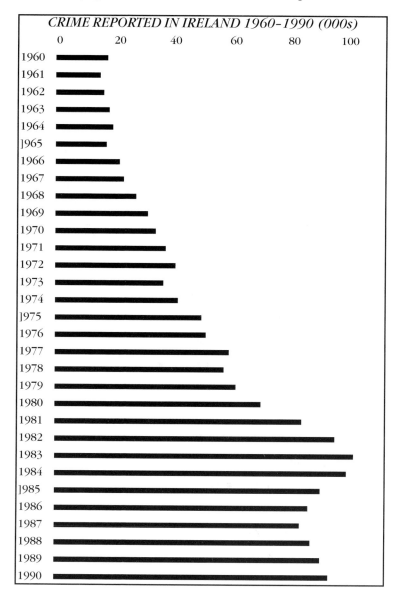

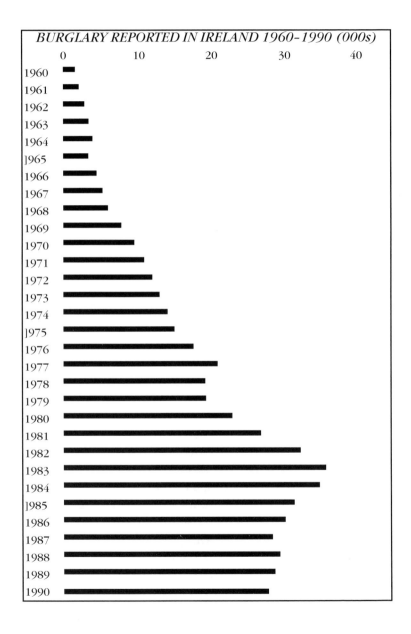

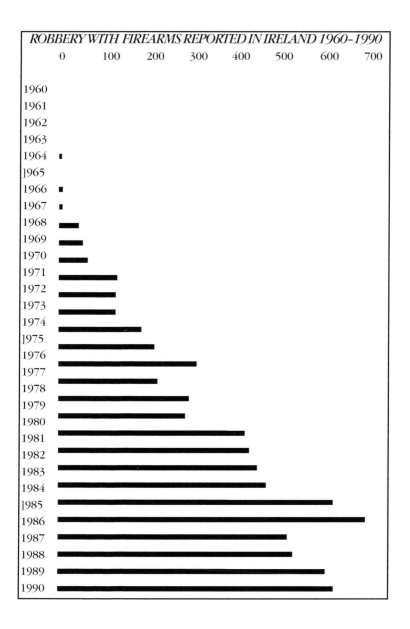

ROBBERY WITH FIREARMS REPORTED IN IRELAND 1960-1990

FAITH AND PEOPLE

Ireland is overwhelmingly Roman Catholic. Though not technically a state religion, the preponderance of Catholicism has exercised a cultural, moral, social and legal influence upon the Irish people for many centuries; it could be argued that the conflicts between the British and the Irish led the Irish to define and identify themselves as a separate people through their church having been denied most forms of political expression.

Economic growth and the close bonds within the European Union with the requirement to align personal rights across a broader canvas have brought about some significant social and legislative changes in recent years. Such changes are bringing Irish practices into line with those generally to be found in Europe, a process that will no doubt continue.

The breakdown of religious affiliation according to the 1991 census was:

Roman Catholic	93.1%
Church of Ireland (Anglican)	2.8%
Presbyterian	0.4%
Others	3.7%

This religious homogeneity means that there is little obvious antipathy to other faiths within the country and also reflects that Ireland has not yet experienced the immigration and accompanying racial mixing and multi-culturalism that has changed British and European society in recent decades.

CHAPTER 3

The Process

As already mentioned, the purpose of this book is to take a systematic look at the whole process of moving home to and settling in Ireland. The problems begin because there are so many things to considerbefore you go: finances, housing, employment, health, education, leisure . . . the list is initially daunting and seems as long as a piece of proverbial string.

We have therefore sought to shuffle all these areas and to collate them into rational groupings that will take you through the planning process. This process falls into five, natural, broad sections:

ARMCHAIR EXPLORATION

This is the easy bit! You are thinking of making a move — possibly it is just an idle dream you have had for years — but you begin to wonder if it really is a practical idea, could you do it? What are you looking for? Do you have any special requirements?

Turn to Chapter 4 for the sort of questions you should be asking yourself.

VISITING AND TOURING

This is the fun part! You have narrowed your choices and defined your basic criteria, but shouldn't you see the places first? Yes, ideally of course you should! You have probably heard those (apocryphal?) tales of people watching an amateur video of some idyllic farmhouse and buying it sight unseen only to find that it is miles up some impassable track, has dreadful damp and five foot high ceilings! Do not take chances. Besides, Ireland is a beautiful country to visit, so pack your bags and go, inspect the areas you had in mind, take note of local house prices first-hand, seek out some local professional firms who could assist with the legal and financial transactions and take note of the local employment opportunities and leisure facilities.

Turn to Chapter 5 for tips and pointers to visiting and touring Ireland.

FINANCIAL PREPARATION

Having made the decision to move, there are a host of financial and legal matters that must be considered and put in order. These could involve resolving your legal status within both Ireland and your original home country, selling or letting your present house, arranging a mortgage, sorting out your pension and tax affairs, plus a host of additional complexities depending on your personal circumstances both at your current address and at your new one in Ireland.

Turn to Chapter 6 for a discussion of financial preparation.

HOUSE BUYING AND MOVING

Now things are really serious. You have done your financial homework, you have found the ideal, general location, you have agents scouring the area contacting you with possible homes and perhaps friends and family on the look out too; it is now just a matter of luck, patience and persistence. Once the deal is done there is the physical move to make, all that sorting, packing and transport to arrange, not forgetting the family pet!

Turn to Chapter 9 for a discussion of house buying and moving.

LIVING THERE

This is why you did it! Beginning to build a new life, joining the local community, enjoying those leisure pursuits that you dreamt of, perhaps starting work or a business or higher education.

Turn to Chapters 10 to 14 for details of living in Ireland.

CHAPTER 4

Armchair Exploration

We are not all natural planners: some of us dream of doing something, but get no further because we only see the problems or are just plain timid. Other people are naturally reckless and simply leap into things, solving problems on the fly and making snap decisions — in other words, hoping for the best.

Spontaneity is a wonderful thing, falling in love, doing something unexpectedly impulsive and out of character. However, moving home, especially to a foreign country, incalculably benefits from a degree of study and soul-searching. This may seem dull and unexciting compared to seeing your dream home and buying it there and then, but such major upheaval and considerable expense does deserve some careful thought and your ultimate decision and enjoyment could be all the better for investing a little time and effort in honing your reasons.

Some of the most significant considerations that will have a bearing on where you chose to live could include the following (and for any family or friends coming to live with you) :

MONEY NEEDS

- What will my income and tax situation be in Ireland?
- Do I need to sell my current home in order to finance my move to Ireland and how much is it worth?
- How much can I afford to spend on a new home in Ireland?
- Can I transfer money freely between countries?
- What will be my tax situation in the UK once I move?
- What are the chances of working in Ireland?
- How can I start my own Business?
- Do I intend to work, if so doing what and are there specific loca-

tions that make this possible (communications, markets, location of firm, business premises, start-up grants)

EDUCATIONAL AND TRAINING NEEDS

- Most importantly, are my current qualifications recognised?
- Do I have any specific educational or training requirements?
- Do I want to pursue my studies in full time/part time adult education?
- What is the local system of nurseries, schools, colleges and universities?

MEDICAL NEEDS

- Do I (or anyone else moving with me) have any specific medical and health requirements? Consider the future as well as the present; perhaps you are fine now, but this could change.
- Do I need specialist medical services or facilities that may only be available at a few centres such as heart, cancer or dialysis treatments amongst others?
- Do I need domestic assistance or nursing care?

MOBILITY

- Do I have restricted mobility (wheelchair user, heart problems, arthritis, impaired vision or any one of many conditions that can limit my ability to get about easily in a strange and unfamiliar environment)?
- Do I need a car and will I always have access to one for shopping and general survival, or for work, education or other leisure interests as well as for emergencies
- Are there good alternatives to a car that meet my needs?

INTERESTS, LEISURE NEEDS

We all realise that when you are considering such a move that employment, healthcare, home buying and such weighty matters are very important, but spare a thought for your particular interest, sport or hobby as these are at least as important

After all you are moving to Ireland to improve your life-style so your leisure time should be factored into the equation when considering where to move to.

So, if you love gardening or watersports you may prefer the south with its palm trees (honest!), lower rainfall and milder climate courtesy of the Gulf Stream. Or perhaps you love museums or theatres which would make a home closer to Dublin more sensible with its easier access to such cultural centres.

The weather is always important, but to generalise, the north tends to experience harsher climes than the south, and the west is wetter than the east.

You should ask yourself, do I have a particular interest that will help to determine my ideal location?
such as:

- Golf
- Fishing
- Sailing/Water Sports
- Horse Racing
- Horse Riding
- Walking/Climbing
- Bird Watching
- Gardens and Gardening
- History/Archaeology
- Architecture/Stately Homes
- Art and Crafts

VIRTUALLY THERE

For those of a technical persuasion the Internet offers considerable opportunity for some 'virtual' exploration from the comfort of your own home.

Simply entering "Ireland' in your search engine will reveal literally thousands of sites covering almost every imaginable facet of Irish life — from the mainstream to the truly off-beat! Enjoy browsing your way through the highways and byways of the world wide web as you follow your personal exploration, and who knows, you could also pick up some invaluable information which may help you to make important decisions about your future.

CHAPTER 5

Visiting and Touring

By now you have started to narrow down your choice of location and the area you have chosen seems to fulfil your requirements (on paper at least.) The next step is to make some arrangements to visit and tour around to check first-hand if it is what you had expected.

When planning a holiday we follow a very standard list of requirements, from accommodation, distance to beach or mountains, local sightseeing, places of interest and leisure facilities. Remember that you can include all these requirements when you plan your visit, but you must start with a different approach. Because time is a very important factor it is important to plan your visit completely. Be careful to maximise your time and money so that having completed your visit you feel that you have achieved enough to bring you nearer to a final decision.

BEFORE YOU GO

Try and gather as much information as possible on all relevant questions to be answered, from medical, employment, education, business, product availability to leisure and relaxation. A lot of the necessary names, addresses and telephone numbers are available within this book.

Make an itinerary so that every day you have contains objectives to achieve. Endeavour to group requirements that are similar, to maximise time and money. Try not to be a tourist; when choosing a bar/restaurant/shop do not go into the ones that are aimed at visitors, but be adventurous and investigate the smaller establishments. The latter are often distinguished by a lack of signs for Special Offers, Set Menus and Traditional Music. Immerse yourself in the local atmosphere and get the feel of the village, town or city.

Above all talk to the natives! If you do you will (very quickly) get to hear all the bad things people feel about their local and national government along with the standing of the local Gaelic Football Team. You may come home with more questions than answers, but you will not be disappointed. You have started the process and because the cost of telephone calls are cheaper now and a lot of information is available in the UK just keep to the task and you will achieve your goal!

PLENTY TO SEE AND DO

Should your dedication to your stated task begin to flag, Ireland has many, many leisure activities and entertainments on offer.

To mention just some of them:

- Beaches, loughs, rivers, boating, sailing and watersports
- Walking, hiking and horse riding
- Shopping, theatres and cinemas
- Pubs, restaurants and bars aplenty, many of international renown
- History, archaeology, architecture and genealogy
- Horse racing
- Sports, especially the uniquely Irish Gaelic football and hurdling, but including rugby, soccer, dog racing and many more
- Golf, now a major industry in its own right
- Fishing, both sea and river
- Arts and crafts
- Music and dance
- Travelling and touring by car, caravan, rail, bus, cycle, pony or foot, following an itinerary or just taking each day as it comes

There's something there for nearly everyone, surely?

ACCESSIBILITY

Over the centuries Ireland has benefited from the various waves of investment that came with each technological advance in transport. Starting with a network of trackways, then canal and river systems, shortly followed by a remarkable railway building bonanza (given the wealth and production of the country), then the upgrading and metalling of the roads and latterly all the modern appurtenances of a successful state: motorways, international airports and fast ferries.

For its size, both geographic and economic, Ireland is extraordinarily well served these days and the visitor should find no difficulty in getting about regardless of the means they prefer or are able to use. The best way to truly enjoy Ireland — unfortunately to the minds of many — is to have access to a car. Even though there is an excellent bus, coach and rail network a car will give you the freedom to enjoy the mountains, the beaches, the lakes and the countryside as well as making light work of heavy shopping.

PASSPORTS

United Kingdom citizens born in the UK and travelling directly from the UK to Ireland do not need a passport. If you are not a UK citizen, whether travelling from the UK or elsewhere in the world, you may well need a passport and even a visa. If there is any element of doubt whatsoever, you should contact your nearest Irish Embassy or Consulate or check with your travel agent or carrier well in advance of your travel date. In the United Kingdom contact:

Irish Embassy
17 Grosvenor Place
London SW1X 7HR
Tel: (0171) 235 2171

DISTANCES

First you must remember that Ireland is a small country and that you are never far from the sea, mountains, city or lakes. You must also remember that apart from main motorways, which are small in number, the main roadways are A and B roads and in most cases are fairly slow and winding, and pass through many small towns where you may find that a couple of farmers have parked their tractors in the middle of the road to pop in to have a pint and a chat.

Fortunately the provision of Irish route signs is increasing, so you should be able to explore with confidence, rather than fear getting lost and being told in that time-honoured Irish way 'I wouldn't start from here!' So always allow extra time for the unexpected, but remember that part of the reason for moving to Ireland is not to zap up and down the motorways and A roads, but to relax, enjoy the scenery and if you are a little late nobody seems to mind, in fact it is half expected.

TABLE OF DISTANCES (MILES) AND TIMES (HOURS) BETWEEN MAJOR IRISH TOWNS

	1 Athlone	2 Cork	3 Donegal	4 Dublin	5 Dundalk	6 Galway	7 Kilkenny	8 Killarney	9 Limerick	10 Roscommon	11 Rosslare Harbour	12 Shannon Airport	13 Sligo	14 Waterford
1 Athlone														
2 Cork	136 / 4½													
3 Donegal	114 / 4	250 / 7½												
4 Dublin	78 / 2½	160 / 4½	138 / 4											
5 Dundalk	90 / 2½	202 / 5½	127 / 3½	53 / 1½										
6 Galway	58 / 1½	130 / 3½	192 / 5½	136 / 4	148 / 4½									
7 Kilkenny	78 / 2½	92 / 2½	253 / 7½	73 / 2	123 / 3½	107 / 3								
8 Killarney	114 / 4½	54 / 1½	184 / 5½	192 / 5½	219 / 6½	120 / 3½	123 / 3½							
9 Limerick	75 / 2½	65 / 2	123 / 3½	123 / 3½	150 / 4½	65 / 2	70 / 2	69 / 2						
10 Roscommon	20 / ½	156 / 4½	94 / 2½	91 / 2½	94 / 2½	51 / 1½	98 / 2½	164 / 4½	94 / 2½					
11 Rosslare Harbour	130 / 3½	129 / 3½	243 / 7	101 / 3	153 / 4½	170 / 5	62 / 1½	171 / 5	131 / 3½	150 / 4½				
12 Shannon Airport	83 / 2½	80 / 2½	176 / 5	138 / 4	165 / 4½	57 / 1½	85 / 2½	84 / 2½	15 / ½	96 / 2½	146 / 4½			
13 Sligo	73 / 2	209 / 6	41 / 1½	135 / 4	104 / 3	86 / 2½	152 / 4½	213 / 6	144 / 4	53 / 1½	203 / 5½	136 / 4		
14 Waterford	108 / 3	78 / 2½	222 / 6½	98 / 3	151 / 4½	137 / 4	30 / 1	80 / 2½	120 / 3½	129 / 3½	51 / 1½	51 / 1½	95 / 2½	
15 Wexford	117 / 3½	116 / 3½	231 / 6½	88 / 2½	141 / 4	157 / 4	50 / 1½	158 / 4½	118 / 3½	138 / 4	12 / ½	133 / 3½	191 / 5½	39 / 1½

SCHEDULED AIR SERVICES TO IRELAND FROM THE UK

From	To	Airline
Birmingham	Dublin	Aer Lingus/Ryanair
Birmingham	Cork	Aer Lingus
Birmingham	Knock	Aer Lingus
Blackpool	Dublin	Air South West
Bouremouth	Dublin	Ryanair
Bristol	Cork	British Airways Express
Bristol	Dublin	Aer Lingus
Cambridge	Waterford	Suckling Airways
East Midlands	Dublin	British Midland
Edinburgh	Dublin	Aer Lingus
Exeter	Dublin	Jersey European Air
Guernsey	Dublin	Jersey European Air
Glasgow	Carrickfinn	British Airways Express
Glasgow	Dublin	Aer Lingus
Glasgow-Prestwick	Carrickfinn	Gill Air
Glasgow-Prestwick	Dublin	Ryanair
Isle of Man	Dublin	Manx Air
Jersey	Cork	ManxAir
Jersey	Dublin	Aer Lingus/Manx Air/Jersey EA
Leeds/Bradford	Dublin	Aer Lingus/Ryanair
Liverpool	Dublin	Ryanair
London-City	Dublin	CityJet
London-Heathrow	Cork	Aer Lingus
London-Heathrow	Dublin	Aer Lingus/British Midland
London-Heathrow	Shannon	Aer Lingus
London-Gatwick	Cork	British Airways Express
London-Gatwick	Dublin	British Airways Express/Ryanair
London-Gatwick	Shannon	AB Shannon
London-Luton	Dublin	Ryanair
London-Luton	Kerry	Manx Air
London-Luton	Waterford	Suckling Airways
London-Stansted	Cork	Ryanair
London-Stansted	Dublin	Ryanair/Aer Lingus
London-Stansted	Knock	Ryanair
London-Stansted	Waterford	British Airways Express
Manchester	Cork	British Airways Express
Manchester	Dublin	Aer Lingus/Ryanair
Manchester	Kerry	British Airways Express
Manchester	Knock	British Airways Express
Manchester	Shannon	British Airways Express
Manchester	Waterford	British Airways Express
Newcastle	Dublin	Aer Lingus
Plymouth	Dublin	Air South West
Plymouth	Cork	British Airways/Air South West

FLIGHTS

With major airports at Dublin, Shannon, Cork and Knock and regional ones at Waterford, Donegal (Carrickfinn), Kerry and Sligo — and Derry and Belfast in the North — nearly every part of Ireland is little more than an hour or two's flight from Britain.

In line with most of Europe, over the past five years the skies have opened up as far as choice of airline and price structures is concerned. Because of this much fiercer competition for your valuable custom, most fares to Ireland are now very reasonable and you will frequently see special offers being advertised in the press. It is certainly worth shopping around for good fares, so check with the 12 airlines whose names are listed below, all of whom fly regularly from mainland Britain to the Republic.

AB Airlines
Enterprise House
Stansted Airport
Essex CM24 1QW
Tel: (0345) 464748

Aer Lingus
83 Staines Road
Hounslow
Middlesex TW3 3JB
London area telephone: (0181) 899 4747
Outside London telephone: (0645) 737 747

Air South West
Cork Airport
Ireland
Tel: (01392) 360772/(1232) 457 200

British Airways Express
British Regional Airlines
Suite 16
Manchester International Office Centre
Styal Road
Manchester M22 5WB

British Midland
Donington Hall
Castle Donington
Derby DE74 2SB
Tel: (0345) 554588

Cityflyer Express
Iain Stewart Centre
Beehive Ring Road
Gatwick RH6 0PB
Tel: (0345) 222111

CityJet
London City Airport
The Royal Docks
London E16 2PX
Tel: (0345) 445588

Gill Airways
Newcastle Airport
New Aviation House
Newcastle Upon Tyne
NE13 8BT
Tel: (0191) 214 6666

Jersey European Airways
Exeter Airport
Devon EX5 2BD
Tel: (0345) 676676

Manx Airlines Ltd
Ronaldsway Airport
Ballasalla
Isle of Man IM9 2JE
Tel: (0345) 256256

Ryanair
Enterprise House

Stansted Airport
Essex CM24 1QW
Tel: (0345) 464748

Suckling Airways
Cambridge Airport
Cambridge CB5 8RT
Tel: (01223) 293 393

It is always wise to book as early as possible to obtain the specific flights you require as well as to obtain the best price. Certain times of year of course, see dramatic increases in traffic, such as at Easter, St. Patrick's Day, and Christmas, when obtaining a flight at short notice can become next to impossible.

See the list on the left for information on the links and servicing airlines that connect Irish airports with mainland Britain. Apart from these links there are a wide selection of flights to European, American and world-wide destinations. For instance Aer Lingus, the national Irish carrier, operates the following services to the United States of America:

From	*To*
Dublin, Shannon	Boston
Dublin, Shannon	Chicago
Dublin, Shannon and Belfast	New York
Dublin, Shannon	Newark

Delta Airlines flies between Shannon and Dublin to Atlanta and New York, and Aer Lingus, Air Inter, Alitalia, Iberia, Lufthansa, Ryanair, Sabena, SAS and TAP all operate scheduled flights from destinations across Europe to Ireland. Always check with your local airline office or travel agent for detailed information.

FERRIES

If you do not wish to fly or want to drive your own vehicle once you arrive in Ireland, then there are a number of ferry routes and operators to choose from. Unlike the airlines there is little competition from new, small niche operators to the established ferry companies. However, the competitive prices and services being offered by the airlines is having a knock-on effect with the ferries who are now setting keener prices and packages. This previous lack of competitive edge also meant that fares tended to be on the high side when compared to the English Channel routes, but this situation is changing, too.

That said, the ferry companies operate a pretty comprehensive set of routes from the west coast of Britain and the Atlantic coast of France, across to destinations in Ireland at Dublin, Dun Laoghaire, Rosslare (Wexford) and Cork and also to Larne and Belfast in the North. A word of caution: ferry services tend to have very seasonal sailing variations so you must check well in advance with the operator or your travel agent.

The warnings on popular and busy travel times that apply to air travel are equally true of the ferries, so plan ahead and book early for those periods.

Ferries to Ireland from Britain

Holyhead/Dun Laoghaire
Stena Line
Charter House
Park Street
Ashford
Kent TN24 8EX
Ferry Reservations: (0990) 707070/(0990) 747474
Service: HSS from 99min; Superferry 3hr 30min

Holyhead/Dublin City (Dublin Ferryport)
Irish Ferries
Reliance House
Water Street
Liverpool L2 8TP
Tel: (0990) 17171
Ferry Enquiries: (0345) 171717/(0990) 170000
Service: 3hr 15min

Fishguard/Rosslare
Stena Line
Service: Lynx from 99min; Superferry 3hr 20min

Pembroke/Rosslare
Irish Ferries
Service: 3hr 45min

Swansea/Cork
Swansea Cork Ferries
Kings Docks
Swansea SA1 8RU
Service: 10hr

Isle of Man/Dublin
Isle of Man Steam Packet Company
PO Box 5
Imperial Buildings
Douglas IM99 1AF
Tel: (01624) 661661
Service: 2hr 45min

Stranraer/Belfast
Stena Line
Service: HSS 105min; Superferry 3hr

Stranraer/Belfast
SeaCat Scotland
West Pier
Stranraer DG9 7RE
Tel: (0345) 523523
Service: 90min

Cairnryan/Larne
P & O European Ferries
Larne Harbour
Larne
Co. Antrim BT40 1AQ
Tel: (0990) 980777
Service: Jetliner 1hr; Ferry 2hr 15min

Liverpool/Belfast
Norse Irish Ferries
North Brocklebank Dock
Bootle
Merseyside L20 1BY
Tel: (01232) 779090
Service: 11hr

ROADS

Ireland has a good road network that has undergone considerable renewal and upgrading in recent years. Roads are categorised according to their importance, capacity and condition:

- 'N' ROADS are the national roads, the major trunk routes, similar in purpose to British 'A' roads.
- MOTORWAYS are a relatively new phenomenon in Ireland. They have often been funded through European Union grants and are being constructed both as entirely new routes and by upgrading existing roads to relieve particular stress points.

If you are not driving your own or a hire car, then there is a good bus and coach network in place to transport you. Often state-owned and run by Coras Iompair Eirann, there are many companies in operation. Most bus and coach companies provide services within and around an urban centre, reaching out to its suburbs and rural hinterland and beyond to the national network. The national operator is Bus Eireann, a reliable company that offers an excellent service with very good country-wide coverage — see the section bow on coaches and buses

Driving

Having mentioned that being able to drive around Ireland is a wonderful way to see the country and to go exploring its remoter nooks and crannies, there are a number of legislative restrictions to pass before you can do so, concerning such matters as your drivers licence and insurance.

The Irish drive on the same side of the road as the British and use very similar road signs. Signposts are often bilingual and despite being adherents of the metric system you will still find road signs giving distances in miles rather than kilometres.

Unleaded petrol is widely available at petrol stations, and just as in Britain and elsewhere, you will find variations in petrol prices from garage to garage. As a general guide you can currently expect to pay the following sorts of prices:

Fuel Type	Price per Litre
Premium Leaded	65
Regular Leaded	60
Super Unleaded	67
Diesel	57

A United Kingdom Driver's Licence should be acceptable for driving in Ireland, at least for vacation purposes or you could get an International Driver's Licence which is usable in Ireland for limited periods.

For longer stays it is feasible to transfer your Australian or some European Community drivers licences straight into an Irish one, but this must be done within one year of your arrival. Holders of United States of America or Canadian licences will have to apply for a separate Irish licence which will involve both practical and oral tests.

Car insurance is compulsory in Ireland, but the size of your premium can be reduced if you are currently benefiting from a no-claims bonus in your existing country provided it has similar insurance laws to Ireland's, such as European Union member states, the United States of America, Australia and Canada. This premium reduction is discretionary and will be granted on a case by case basis and only then on production of supporting documentary evidence.

Most UK insurance company's policies will cover you whilst driving in Ireland, but you must inform them of your trip before departure and have this confirmed.

Motor Tax is also levied in Ireland at rates that vary according to the size of your car. This tax can be paid quarterly, half yearly or annually.

Motor Tax Office
Department of the Environment
Tel: (01) 872 0077

The wearing of seat belts is compulsory for drivers and front seat passengers and children under the age of 12 are not allowed to travel in front seats. Motor cyclists and their passengers must wear helmets.

You should also be aware that it is illegal for an Irish resident to drive your car unless they be a garage mechanic who has your written permission.

Car Hire

It goes without saying, which is why we repeat it here, that you will need a current driver's licence issued by your country of residence, but in addition you must have held it for at least two years and be free of endorsements.

Because of very high insurance premiums and the fact that all of Ireland's cars and spare parts are imported, car hire can be expensive. All the major car hire companies are represented and there are a number of local companies, too, so if you shop around you should be able to get a good deal. Also most airline and ferry companies have special rates for their passengers — so ask.

Always check whether the rates are for unlimited mileage or if it is for a stated distance with an extra charge for each additional mile thereafter, as this latter can also prove expensive, especially if you intend to drive many miles. Also check if you intend to fly into one airport and out from another as some hire companies do not allow this or there maybe an extra charge.

Insurance conditions on hire cars tend to be stiffer than for owner drivers and in Ireland you will usually only be able to get hire car insurance if you are between the ages of 24 and 69, but this can vary, so do shop around.

Some useful addresses:

Avis Rent-A-Car Ltd
1 Hanover Street East
Dublin 2
Tel: (01) 677 4010
Budget Rent-A-Car
Dublin Airport
Tel: (01) 8445 919

Flynn Brothers
Ballygar
County Galway
Tel: (0903) 24668

Hertz Rent-A-Car
Dublin Airport
Tel: (01) 8445466

Murrays Europcar
Baggot Street Bridge
Dublin 4
Tel: (01) 668 1777

The Car Rental Council
5 Upper Pembroke Street
Dublin 2
Tel: (01) 676 1690

Buses and Coaches

There are two main Irish bus operators: Dublin Bus and Irish Bus, with Dublin Bus operating in Dublin City and surrounding areas, and Irish Bus operating a nation-wide service and some city-based networks.

Dublin Bus (*Bus Atha Cliath*) operate a network of bus routes throughout Dublin with the city centre as their main hub, so that to make a journey, say, from a south-east suburb to a south-west one will probably be quickest by going into the centre and out again — annoying, but you will see plenty of Dublin's architecture as you travel about!

There are also the Nitelink Buses for party-goers and night-lifers which run until 2.00am. Always enquire after the wide range of discounted fares available. Tickets can be bought at over 200 agencies across the region or from Dublin Bus direct:

Dublin Bus Head Office
59 Upper O'Connell Street
Dublin 1
Tel: (01) 873 4222 *for passenger information*

Irish Bus *(Bus Eireann)* operates the country-wide network which, as implied, reaches all corners of the country, is regular, competitively priced and reasonably comfortable as well as the regional services centred on Cork, Galway, Limerick and Waterford.

Check for details of special offers, rover tickets and discounts for the elderly as these will frequently be available and can represent major savings compared to standard, daily fares.

Bus Eireann Travel Centre
Central Bus Station
Store Street
Dublin 1
Tel: (01) 836 6111 *for passenger information*

Apart from these main, state-owned bus companies, there are the private coach companies offering a variety of routes, services and private hire.

RAILWAYS

As in Britain, there was a late nineteenth century railway building boom that bequeathed Ireland a remarkably comprehensive rail network. Though in modern times the system has been nationalised, and is nowadays known as Irish Rail or *Iarnrod Eireann* and has been severely pruned with many branch lines being closed, there remains an efficient and eminently useable railway network that connects the major centres within the country.

Dublin, which does not possess an underground railway system, does have the Dublin Area Rapid Transit (DART) rail system which operates along the Dublin regional eastern coastline connecting 25 railway stations from Howth in the north down to Bray in the south, and which is fast and efficient and provides a regular service.

As with the buses, check for special tickets and offers.

Iarnrod Eireann
Connolly Station
Dublin 1
Tel: (01) 836 6222 *for passenger information (including DART)*

IRISH RAILWAY SYSTEM

CANALS AND RIVERS

During the eighteenth and early nineteenth centuries Ireland's natural loughs and waterways were improved for navigation. They were connected by a series of canals that now form a wonderful leisure resource as they wend their way through some of the most beautiful back-country.

WALKING AND CYCLING

With its acres of rolling countryside and miles of quiet country lanes and frequent village pubs, Ireland is an ideal place for walking and cycling. Information for walkers and cyclists can be obtained from the Irish Tourist Board or:

Walking Cycling Ireland
PO Box 5520
Ballsbridge
Dublin 4
Tel: (01) 668 8278
Fax: (01) 660 5566

TOURIST GUIDE BOOKS

As with most countries a large selection of books are available from the detailed to the frivolous, so a visit to your local book store should provide you with a comprehensive selection amongst which at least one will probably serve your particular needs.

HOTELS, GUEST HOUSES AND BED & BREAKFASTS

One thing was always guaranteed when you visited Ireland — you were always assured of a warm welcome and a hearty Irish breakfast (like a full English breakfast, but more!) from Irish hotel, guest house, and bed and breakfast operators down the years.

Apart from the larger, high quality hotel chains and the established, family run hotels, facilities, decor and comfort could all be found wanting until recently. But with the enormous increase in the number of tourists in recent years, the whole industry has been transformed, with the emphasis on service, top quality food, comfortable and modern surroundings, access to IT equipment and many hotels now adding leisure facilities such as swimming pools, gyms and saunas.

Remember, if you feel you need to visit Ireland on more than one occasion your hotel costs could be quite considerable, so bear in mind that quite apart from considerations of cost, you will find out more about your particular area by staying in farmhouse or small bed & breakfast accommodation. There you can talk to people about everyday matters — housing, cost of living, food and shopping, taxes — person to person as opposed to one of the larger hotels where very often the staff are too busy, or always remember you are a 'customer' and treat you as such.

SEASONS TO GO

Whenever anybody speaks of Ireland they always mention the weather, especially the rain - 'It didn't rain at all' (my God) — 'It rained every day for a while'— 'It never stopped'. As the saying has it, 'I went to Ireland for a week and it only rained twice, once for four days and once for three!'

Everybody has their favourite season and Ireland with its varied landscape and coastline has much to offer, from the hot summer's day lying on a sandy beach with a gentle breeze to the wild, January day standing on the cliff's edge with the Atlantic gales whipping the waves to frenzy as they crash against the cliffs, sending up clouds of spray and spume. So the choice is yours, but remember that at Christmas, Easter, Irish Bank Holidays, July and August and times of special sporting fixtures, travel and accommodation costs increase dramatically, flights and ferries are heavily booked and accommodation harder to find; so if you can, try to avoid these dates and book in advance.

Public Holidays
- New Year's Day (1 January)
- St Patrick's Day (17 March)
- Easter Monday
- May Day (First Monday in May)
- First Monday in June
- First Monday in August
- Last Monday in October
- Christmas Day (25 December)
- St Stephen's Day (26 December)

CHAPTER 6

Financial Preparation

Although it is not the purpose of this book to be a definitive legal text nor a comprehensive do-it-yourself taxation guide, it is the intention to highlight and bring to the reader's attention some of the more important matters that they should consider when weighing up the pros and cons of moving home to the Republic of Ireland. You really cannot do too much preparatory work on your finances; you have to consider short and long term financial issues — your income, your capital and its investment, property, wills, changes in rates of exchange, interest rate movements, borrowings, the effect of moving on pensions and taxation on everything! We shall examine the long term and short term issues separately but first of all, there are a number of general points to note:

MOVING MONEY

As part of the European Community there is no hindrance on moving funds between the United Kingdom and Ireland. Matters are made even simpler as the major Irish banks have branches in the UK which makes these transactions easier.

This same ease of transfer applies to all transactions between European Union member states, but for countries outside this zone there may well be restrictions on such cash movements. Obviously you should be aware of any restrictions that pertain to your own particular country and make sure that you comply with them.

VALUE ADDED TAX

Some overseas readers of this book, especially Americans, may not be aware of just what Value Added Tax is so a short description seems in order, but take care as those of us in Europe who have lived with VAT for many years know that its simple theory belies an extraordinarily complex system of operational directives.

The easiest way to think of it is as a glorified sales tax which is charged on every transaction within the supply chain that delivers goods and services to the consumer. If you are legally required or voluntarily able to register as a taxable entity (i.e.) a business of some kind) then the tax you pay on buying goods and services can be offset against the tax you collect by selling them, so that at each stage of the chain only the balance is accountable to the revenue authorities. At the end of the chain comes the one-sided transaction when the person- in-the-street (who cannot register!) buys the goods and services and becomes the ultimate tax payer funding the entire system.

As an American you would be a non-European Union citizen and thus may be able to some relief from paying the tax when buying goods in Ireland. Ask the retailer or look out for 'tax free shopping' signs.

PENSIONS

Living or working overseas for extended periods can seriously affect your pension entitlements. The exact nature of the consequences depends on the nature of your pension arrangements.

If you are a member of a company pension scheme and your employer dispatches you abroad then you will almost certainly be entitled to continue without interruption, though the Inland Revenue remain the final arbiter of such matters.

If you have a personal pension then things are different because you can only make pension contributions from relevant UK earnings, and by definition if you cease to be a UK Resident, then you have no relevant UK earnings from which to make these contributions.

Pensions are a complicated area of financial management and you should speak to your pensions advisor for specific advice relating to your own circumstances.

SELLING/RENTING YOUR ORIGINAL HOME
Selling

This applies to those who will be selling their UK property primarily in order to finance their purchase in Ireland and perhaps also to provide some surplus to fund their new-found lifestyle; if the property in question is your principle residence in the United Kingdom then it would not normally be subject to Capital Gains Tax.

One imagines that most people are familiar with the tortuous and hair-greying UK house selling process and it is not really within the scope of this book to explore this particular topic further. See your local estate agent for details.

Renting

Those who have sufficient means to buy another property whilst keeping their UK home intact may decide to let their original home. If you intend to do this you must notify any mortgage holders or lenders with loans secured on it (since they will have lent on the understanding that this was to be a domestic property rather than an income earning asset that it is now effectively to become) as well as your insurers since the nature of the occupancy and risks involved will be changing.

As for property letting, a good agent to look after your interests, keep a watch on the property and most importantly to find a steady flow of reliable tenants whilst you live abroad is clearly a sensible option, though not essential. They will also be able to advise you through the complications of Assured and Assured Shorthold Tenancies and the regulations of the several Housing and Landlord & Tenant Acts.

Rental income from a United Kingdom property is subject to UK income tax, or more accurately the net profits from the rental after allowing for agent's fees, wear and tear and so forth. In fact matters go further in that rents paid to an overseas landlord are required to have tax deducted at source and the tenant, or agent if there is one, is required to pay this deducted tax to the Inland Revenue on a quarterly basis. To gain exemption from having this tax withheld you must file a Form NRL 1 with the UK revenue authorities which requires the landlord to submit an annual tax return and confirm that they will pay any UK taxes as they fall due.

If you are living abroad and now letting what was formerly your principle residence in the UK it could fall foul of Capital Gains tax if you chose to sell it. The tax will normally be assessed on the period during which it was not your principle residence. If you return from abroad and take up residence in the property again it remains fully outside the scope of Capital Gains Tax.

The above comments on Capital Gains Tax only superficially touch on what is a very complicated area of taxation and are only included to point you at some possible problems and are not intended as a definitive statement of practice or law. As considerable sums of money are involved you are strongly advised to seek professional advice on the precise regulations affecting your personal situation and the correct means to minimise any liability.

LONG TERM FINANCIAL ISSUES
Personal Taxation Status

The key financial concern you will have in your move concerns taxation. Will you be taxed in the United Kingdom or in Ireland? Taxation is a complicated matter, so it has been covered in two sections. This chapter focuses on where you will pay tax and the United Kingdom issues. Income tax relating to the Republic of Ireland has been covered separately in Chapter 10.

This is the moment to introduce some legal terms and definitions that will have a marked bearing on your financial affairs especially where they cross the desk of the ever vigilant tax collector. Assuming that you are a United Kingdom citizen and are currently living in the UK then the Inland Revenue will be chasing you at the very least for Income Tax on your income arising in the UK, Income Tax on income arising outside the UK, Capital Gains Tax and Inheritance Tax and once you move to Ireland you will have the Irish revenue authorities equally as keen to dip into your bottomless pocket and tap your limitless wealth. If you are Resident in Ireland for a given tax year then normally you will be taxed in Ireland according to local practice on all of your income whether it is derived from within Ireland or from overseas and you will normally be entitled to the full range of allowances that can reduce the tax burden.

Double Taxation

The very real danger arises from the fact that if you work and earn abroad you will probably be taxed on those earnings according to that country's system, a system which may well involve taxing you on your world-wide income regardless of origin. If you are not abroad for long enough the UK tax man will not regard you as being non-resident for UK tax purposes and will proceed to tax you on those same earnings as well as on your UK derived income, investments, etc., as normal. This dire phenomenon is known as Double Taxation.

Fortunately Ireland and the United Kingdom have signed a Double Taxation Treaty to rationalise the situation and eliminate the worst effects of this nightmare scenario. In fact at the end of 1997 Ireland had a number of such treaties involving the following countries: Australia, Austria, Belgium, Canada, Cyprus, Czech Republic, Denmark, Finland, France, Germany, Hungary, Israel, Italy, Japan, Korea, Luxembourg, Netherlands, New Zealand, Norway, Pakistan, Poland, Portugal, Russia, Spain, Sweden, Switzerland, United Kingdom, United States of America and Zambia.

The key issue in taxation is the question of residency.

STATUS

'Resident', 'Ordinarily Resident', 'Domicile' and 'Citizen' are terms that often get banded about or thrown gratuitously into explanatory paragraphs. This is dangerous as they have exacting legal definitions that can have an important impact on your life, so I am afraid that we are going to have to attempt to gain some understanding of their particular legalistic meanings.

Sadly things can get yet more complicated because, from the standpoint of this book, you are having to deal with at least two separate taxing regimes, that of your current residence and that of Ireland. If you are a United Kingdom citizen and have lived and paid taxes in the UK for many years past, you will be aware of self assessment — the new and rigorous system of Self Assessment Tax Returns that now operates in the UK. The Self Assessment form has sections that cover people moving abroad for extended periods and failure to submit the properly completed forms and to settle any taxes due by the specified dates (31 January for the annual tax return) will now incur automatic financial penalties and interest charges. It is therefore important not to neglect this requirement. To help you complete your forms correctly the Inland Revenue issue a number of explanatory leaflets some of which relate to overseas employment:

- IR20 Residents and Non-Residents
- IR58 Going to Work Abroad?
- IR300 Non-Residents and Investment Income
- IR302 Dual Residents

Resident

In simplistic terms this means to the tax authorities the same as it means in common usage, that is, the location where you live. Since this is where you live it is logically the place where you pay your taxes. But why would you not want to maintain your UK resident status? Well, as a non-resident you will not be liable to pay UK taxes on any of your income that comes from outside the UK even if it is paid in the UK or transferred here. Another major advantage is that provided you maintain your non-resident status for at least three years you will not pay UK Capital Gains Tax on any dealings made in the UK or abroad between the date of your original departure and the date of your final return.

So, if you move abroad you will probably not wish to continue paying United Kingdom taxes and if you can obtain your non-resident status you will generally not be liable to. There are, though, sev-

AM I RESIDENT OR NON-RESIDENT IN THE UK?

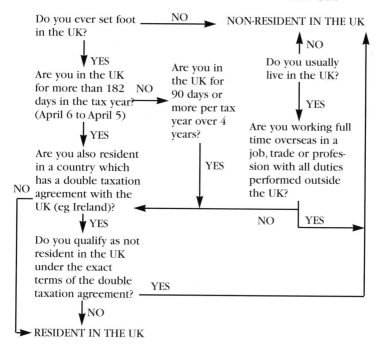

eral conditions that must be met to maintain or break this condition and it is easier to think in the negative — what must I do in order not to be resident for taxation purposes.

The important thing to bear in mind is that we are dealing with UK tax years that run from 6 April of one year to 5 April of the next and not some other randomly chosen period of 12 months.

If you are living outside the United Kingdom for a full tax year then you are no longer legally Resident here with the provisos that you must not visit the United Kingdom for more than 182 days in any particular tax year nor, as an average, visit the United Kingdom for more than 90 days in any particular tax year across a four year period. Special rules apply to certain Crown employees such as members of the diplomatic service and armed forces who will not usually lose their Resident status when abroad.

It is the time spent abroad that matters, not whether you own houses or other property in the UK and you should also remember that Residence is assessed separately on husbands and wives

In broad outline you will be considered Resident in Ireland for a given tax year only if you meet one of these two criteria:

- You spent more than 183 days in the Republic of Ireland during that year
- You spent more than 280 days in the Republic of Ireland during that and the preceding year together, unless you spent less than 30 days in Ireland in one of those years in which case for that particular year you would not be considered Resident

Ordinarily Resident

This denotes a level of residence that has become habitual and is more permanent than the lesser Resident status. The point being that you will remain liable to pay Irish taxes even if you leave the country for occasional periods of residence elsewhere.

You will be classed as Ordinarily Resident in the Republic of Ireland for a given tax year if you have been Resident for each of the preceding three years and you only stop being Ordinarily Resident after three consecutive years of not having Resident status.

Domicile

Domicile is utterly distinct from both Residence or Nationality and although it is possible to be Resident in more than one country you can only have one Domicile.

Generally speaking it is the legal system in which you are deemed to have your permanent home that governs your Domicile. Your children acquire their Domicile from their parents and this will stay with them unless as an adult they gain a Domicile of their own.

Domicile matters because it has a bearing on Inheritance Tax which remains payable on your estate even though you are a Non-Resident for other taxation purposes.

To establish a new Domicile, one outside the United Kingdom in this case, you have to establish that you have made a permanent move abroad by doing such things as taking up local Citizenship, becoming strongly economically involved there, perhaps by building up a commercial enterprise, sending your children to school in your new country and generally breaking all your links and ties with the UK.

Even once the authorities recognise your new Domicile you will still have to see out three years before Inheritance Tax no longer applies to your entire estate, though it will still come into play on any assets that you continue to hold in the United Kingdom.

Citizenship and Nationality

Your Nationality is derived from the sovereign state to which you belong. In Ireland Citizenship is governed by the 'Irish Nationality and Citizenship Act, 1956'. In broad terms you qualify as an Irish citizen if you are born in Ireland, if your parents were born there or possibly if one of your grandparents was born there.

Non-Residents

If you are a Non-Resident, that is you have failed to meet any of the aforementioned criteria, then only your income derived from sources within the Republic of Ireland will be subject to Irish taxation. As a general rule such people are not eligible to claim the various tax allowances that can reduce this burden, though there are, you guessed it, exceptions to this general rule such as for Irish Citizens or a person previously Resident who has been forced to move abroad for the sake of their health or that of a member of their family.

As you will have observed from the above outlines, despite a deliberate effort to make these concepts understandable and to demonstrate how they can affect the person-in-the-street as they go about their lives, we are dealing here with critical definitions and precise criteria that must be complied with in full in order to assess your true legal status for taxation purposes. Given their crucial nature and the fiendish complexity of taxation statutes we cannot emphasise enough that if you are in any doubt or wish to make any financial plans of even a moderate nature, or even if you think that you are doing the correct thing already, you really should seek professional, skilled advice from an experienced practitioner in these matters. Sound advice now could save heartache and financial loss later — the fees involved would be a good investment.

SHORT TERM FINANCIAL ISSUES

You need to tell various agencies, institutions and other concerns that you are going and when you are leaving. If you are moving abroad for either an extended period or permanently, whether to Ireland or to any other part of the globe, then there are a number of administrative actions that you should fulfil, primarily informing the various financial and taxation agencies of your changing circumstances. The most important are examined below.

When writing to these various government agencies always include your National Insurance Number as this will greatly facilitate their handling your affairs and ensure that they are dealing with the correct individual.

Income Tax office

The office that currently handles your affairs will either be the one that you have been submitting tax returns to directly or else the one with whom your employer is registered. They will need to know the precise date of your leaving the United Kingdom and the country to which you are going.

Contributions Agency

The Contributions Agency that collects and records your National Insurance contributions will also need to know the date of your departure and your destination. The correct handling of your contributions is important as some state benefits are directly linked to the amount and history of your payments into the system.

Contributions Agency
Longbenton
Newcastle-upon-Tyne
NE98 1YX

Benefits Agency

The Benefits Agency will need to know that you are moving, especially if you are receiving any benefits as you could cease to be eligible to receive some benefits or may find that they are frozen in value at the level prevailing at your departure. Furthermore, those to which you are still entitled to will need to be directed to an appropriate address.

Benefits Agency Pensions and Overseas Benefits Directorate
Tyneview Park
Newcastle-upon-Tyne
NE98 1BA

MOTORING MATTERS

- *United Kingdom Driving Licence*
  It would be sensible to maintain this as it is both recognised in many other countries (check before you go!) so permitting you to drive there at least for a limited period, during which you will most likely have to obtain a local licence, and because you may be returning to the United Kingdom either for good or periodically.
  You may also find it advantageous to obtain an International Driving Permit. These are valid for one year, but only outside the issuing country so make sure to obtain one before you leave the UK. In the UK both the Automobile Association (AA) and Royal Automobile Club (RAC) can issue these to members and non-members alike.

RAC Travel Services
PO Box 1500
Bristol BS99 2LH

Automobile Association: check your local telephone directory for your nearest office

- *Vehicle Licence*
  When you take your private car overseas for a period exceeding one year the authorities in the United Kingdom regard this as a Permanent Export and you should either apply to a local Vehicle Registration Office for the necessary form or complete the Permanent Export part of your vehicle's existing registration document; either way the completed paperwork has to be sent to the DVLC.

  Driver and Vehicle Licensing Centre
  Swansea
  SA99 1AB

- *Vehicle Insurance*
  Let your insurer know of your movements in order to ensure that your United Kingdom coverage can be cancelled and appropriate coverage arranged for your new destination. You may have to arrange your overseas insurance through a local company.

OTHER MATTERS

It is remarkable how complex has become the web of organisations upon which our lives depend. There are now a host of people all of whom will need to know of your move. These include:

- Your Bank and Building Society Manager
- Financial and Professional Advisors such as solicitor and accountant, investment and insurance brokers (or if you have no advisors this should cover such items as your Pension Company, Life, Health and General Insurance Companies),
- National Savings Office
- The Registrar of any corporation whose stocks and shares you own
- Doctor, Dentist and Optician
- The Utilities (telephone, cable TV provider, gas, electricity, water — leaving time for systems to be closed down and meters read)

- The local Council (for Council Tax)
- Credit and Debit Card Issuers (general and store cards)
- Rental and Hire Purchase Companies
- Your Mortgage Lender
- Your Landlord if renting
- Plus any regular orders you may have such as for milk and paper deliveries
- Memberships and Subscriptions
- Mobile Telephone provider
- And no doubt others particular to your own circumstances.

CHAPTER 7

The Euro

At the time of writing European Monetary Union is well on target. Ireland, as a fervent supporter of the European project, is to be amongst the first wave of entrants to sign up and this will see the Irish Punt replaced by the Euro from 1st January 1999.

The United Kingdom has so far opted for a policy of wait-and-see and has reserved its right to join the EMU at a later date of its own choosing once the UK economic cycle is more in sync with that of the major mainland European economies.

The implications for the UK are well outside the province of this book and as for Ireland a lot depends on the exchange rate of Punts to Euros that is agreed as this rate once set is irrevocable. Linked to that is the likely movement in interest rates once setting them becomes the domain of the European Central Bank rather than that of the Irish government.

Because of its largely unrecognised importance to people and business in Ireland, we have devoted this chapter to a detailed and almost technical description of the implications of European Monetary Union. This information has been supplied courtesy of the Bank of Ireland. Remember, however, that opinions expressed and estimates given are for information only and subject to change without notice.

INTRODUCTION

Over the next two years Ireland will embrace two unique events — the Millennium and EMU. Both very different but both equally important. Most people are thinking of, or planning for, the Millennium — where will they be, who with, what party or city should they go to. No doubt that there is going to be one big party right across the world. EMU on the other hand has not quite worked people into such an excited state (unless you are a banker) — but it is coming and every one should understand how it will affect them and in particular people in business no matter how large or small. Over the next few years businesses must prepare (no business is exempt) as EMU will affect all of them in some shape or form and companies need to start planning now. The effects of EMU will begin to impact on companies from the 1st of January, 1999, but companies must be prepared for complete conversion by 2002 at the latest. The key areas of impact are strategy and communications, information technology, sales and marketing, human resources and training, accounting and finance and legal issues.

We feel that understanding EMU is vitally important for your move and investment in Ireland.

BACKGROUND

Economic and Monetary Union (EMU), which is set to begin on the 1 January 1999, involves the introduction of a single currency called the Euro. As of this May the participating countries are known:

- Austria
- Belgium
- Finland
- France
- Germany
- Ireland
- Italy
- Luxembourg
- Netherlands
- Portugal
- Spain

This leaves out the United Kingdom, Denmark and Sweden by choice, and Greece through failing to meet the required qualifying conditions.

The political leaders of Ireland have been consistently and firmly committed to managing the Irish economy to ensure that Ireland met the convergence criteria. These criteria were focused on the stability of:

- Public Finances
- Exchange Rates
- Interest Rates
- Prices/Inflation

In practical terms, EMU means that the foreign exchange and monetary policies of participating countries will in future be managed by a European Central Bank based in Frankfurt.

EMU TIMETABLE
1998
- In early May, the EU council will decide on the first wave of EMU participants and on the bilateral exchange rates between them which will be used to set the fixed Euro conversion rates to be used from 1 January 1999.
- The European Central Bank will be established in Frankfurt in the weeks following the confirmation of the initial EMU participants.

1999
- The conversion rates between the existing currencies of partici pating countries and the Euro will be irrevocably fixed on 1 January.
- The Euro will exist as a currency but not as cash (i.e. notes and coins.)
- New Irish Government debt will be issued in Euros and existing Irish Government debt will be converted to Euros on the 1st of January.
- All dealings by the Irish Central Bank will be done in Euros.
- The Dublin Interbank, money and bond markets will largely con vert to Euros.
- The Irish Stock Exchange will quote, trade and settle in Euros.
- Transactions by Irish businesses will increasingly use the Euro rather than the national currencies participating in EMU.
- Personal transactions in Ireland will remain largely in Irish Punts.
- Public sector will accept payments in Euros, make payments in Euros if requested, will continue to pay welfare benefits, salaries, wages and pensions in Irish Punts.
- Irish Revenue Commission will accept tax returns in Euros, if the taxpayer wishes.

Transitional Period 1999-2002
During this period businesses will be free to convert some or all of their operations to Euros and to carry out non-cash financial

transactions in Euros. They will not be obliged to do so, however, until January, 2002.

2002

- Euro notes and coins will be introduced from January the 1st.
- Irish Punts will be withdrawn from circulation as quickly as possible.
- All non-cash transactions will be through the Euro rather than through the participating currencies.
- All bank accounts previously denominated in Irish Punts or other participating national currencies will be converted to Euros from January the 1st.
- Businesses which have not already done so will have to convert their financial operations and asset/liability values into Euros.
- Public sector will make all payments, including welfare benefits, salaries, wages and pensions in Euros.

BUSINESS AND THE EURO: QUESTIONS & ANSWERS

Q*: Will the arrival of the Euro have implications for all businesses?*

A: Yes, every business will be affected to a greater or lesser extent. It is essential that each business understands the competitive, commercial, operational and legal implications for its particular activities and plans the necessary responses in a timely fashion. The planning strategy should aim to:

- Maximise business opportunities (procurement and/or sales)
- Address potential new competitive threats
- Manage the transition to Euro in the most cost effective way
- Promote productivity and customer relations

The essential first step to business is to identify responsibility at senior level for the development and co-ordinated implementation of an appropriate EMU-related plan.

Q: *Must businesses be in a position to deal with Euro as well as Irish Punts from 1 January 1999?*

A: Yes, the Euro will be a currency from 1 January 1999 and will be available for use in non-cash form in Ireland and in other countries participating in EMU. From that time, therefore, businesses may be invoiced in Euros by one or more of their suppliers, or may be offered payment in Euros by one or more of their customers. Such suppliers and/or customers could be located in Ireland, in another participating country, or even in a country not participating in EMU.

A number of multi-national corporations have indicated their intention to make and receive business payments in Euros from 1 January 1999. It is likely that their lead will be followed by some other large corporations. It is not possible to predict with any accuracy how quickly the use of the Euro for business payments in Ireland will gather pace after 1 January 1999. All businesses should, therefore, examine whether and how, their systems can cope with incoming and outgoing Euro payments from 1 January 1999 if the need arises. This is particularly important where payment systems are integrated with automated stock control, reconciliation or cash flow management systems.

Q: *Will Businesses have to open Euro bank accounts too make or receive Euro payments?*
A: No, banks will be able to assist businesses in making payments in Euros or in lodging payments in Euros to accounts which remain denominated in Irish Punts. However, businesses will need to consider carefully the implications for their bank reconciliation systems.

Q: *Can businesses be forced to use Euros from 1 January 1999?*
A: No. the legal framework for introduction of the Euro contains a 'no compulsion, no prohibition' principle, which will be in force during the EMU transitional period which will run from 1 January 1999–1 January, 2002. This principle means that no party will be compelled to use the Euro during this period. At a minimum, however, businesses need to consider how they will respond after 1 January 1999:
- If important customers ask to be invoiced in Euros
- If important customers pay in Euros, although invoiced in Irish Punts or other participating currencies
- If one or more of their suppliers invoice them in Euros

Q: *When should businesses approach their software suppliers?*
A: Modern business systems are critically dependent on the ability of their software to adapt to changes in the commercial environ-

ment. The arrival of EMU will involve significant change for most businesses and for many this change will be effective from 1 January 1999. It is essential, therefore, that businesses develop an understanding of what these changes will mean, and how their software suppliers intend to adapt to them. As EMU will start in less than seven months, businesses which have not already done so should approach their software suppliers immediately to identify what EMU-related plans they have and to evaluate the extent to which these plans will satisfy their particular and specific needs. Some businesses may be forced to seek alternative software suppliers if they are not satisfied that their existing suppliers can meet their post-EMU requirements.

Q: *What will EMU mean for business pricing?*
A: There may be a requirement to display prices in both Irish Punts and Euros for a period before and after the introduction of Euro notes and coins, which is scheduled to commence from 1 January, 2002 at the latest. Even if this dual display of prices is not mandatory some businesses, particularly those in the retail sector, may wish to do so to help their customers develop an understanding of the relative values of the new and old currencies. In some business sectors, prices and product characteristics are set at particular 'psychological' points (eg IR£29.99.) Such businesses will need to carefully consider the implications of Euro conversion for their pricing and related strategies.

For fiscal, labour cost, and other traditional reasons, Euro prices for comparable products in countries participating in EMU will not fully converge after 1 January 1999. Such price differences will, however, become more transparent - another important planning consideration for businesses trading with other EMU countries.

Q: *When should businesses change their accounts to Euros?*
A: It will be mandatory to express business accounts in Euros for financial and tax purposes from 1 January, 2002. Businesses can opt to prepare their accounts in Euros during the period between 1 January 1999–January, 2002 if they so wish. Based on its particular circumstances each business must reach its own decision on when it will be most advantageous for it to convert its accounting to Euros.

Some businesses, especially those trading with other EMU countries, may decide there is advantage in converting their accounts during this period in order to simplify internal accounting, to facilitate treasury management, to present a progressive 'European' image and/or to minimise their reliance on scarce IT resources in the lead up to the obligatory changeover to the Euro from 1 January, 2002. Other businesses, particularly those whose trade is largely domestic and/or cash based, will decide to delay changing their accounts until they have to.

The European Commission published a document (numbered XV/7002/97) in June 1997 entitled *Accounting for the Introduction of the Euro*, describing the accounting issues raised by the changeover to Euro.

Q: *Are there tax implications arising from EMU?*
A: In general, the authorities intend that EMU should be as tax neutral as possible. However, issues will arise for some businesses in relation to certain matters, such as the treatment of currency gains/losses which will crystallise when the exchange rates of particular currencies are irrevocable fixed on 1 January 1999 and the depreciation of certain assets whose productive life may be curtailed as a result of the introduction of the Euro (eg vending machines).

The revenue commissioners have produced a booklet outlining their approach to the introduction of the Euro. It is available from:

EMU Unit
Revenue Commissioners
Castle House
South Great George's Street
Dublin 2
Tel (01) 679 2777.

It is important that businesses initiate early discussions with their Bankers, Accountants, Tax Advisors and Legal Advisors to identify and plan for the implications of EMU for their particular commercial operations. It is also important that businesses co-ordinate their plans with those of their major suppliers and customers.

PERSONAL AND BUSINESS BANKING
WITH THE EURO

EMU will start on 1 January 1999 when exchange rates between participating currencies will be irrevocably fixed. Businesses will require some or all of the following services from their banks after 1 January 1999.

- The ability to hold some or all bank accounts in Euros
- The ability to receive payment in Euros
- The ability to make payments in Euros
- Electronic funds transfer

Banks will be in a position to support you in these requirements from 1 January 1999.

Holding Accounts in Euros

Some or all of your bank accounts may be expressed in Euros if you wish. A full range of accounts will be available in Euros including current accounts, loan accounts, saving accounts, etc. . . .

Your branch will be in a position to open new Euro accounts for you or to convert your existing accounts expressed in Irish Punts or other participating currencies to Euros. Such conversions will be carried out free of charge.

Receiving Payment in Euros

You may receive non-cash payments (cheques, transfers) in Euros. Your branch will be in a position to credit these payments to your accounts whether your accounts remain in Irish Punts or are expressed in Euros. Where you receive cash or non-cash payments in Irish Punts or in other participating currencies your branch will be in a position to credit them to your accounts whether your accounts remain in Irish Punts or are expressed in Euros. Domestic or international electronic payments received for your accounts will where necessary be automatically converted to the currency in which your account is held.

Making Payments in Euros

You will be able to pay creditors in Euros whether your accounts are expressed in Euros or in Irish Punts. A full range of payment instruments (including cheque books, electronic payments, drafts etc. . .) will be available from your branch in Euros regardless of whether your account is in Irish Punts or Euros.

Electronic Funds Transfer
You will be able to originate direct debits or make electronic payments in Euros through the electronic funds transfer system without regard to whether the payer or beneficiary accounts are expressed in Euros or in Irish Punts.

Other Facilities
The bank will print the Euro equivalent balance on all statements issued for accounts which remain expressed in Irish Punts or in another participating currency. If you require, your branch will be able to provide you with mortgages, lifetime policies, leases etc., expressed in Euros. You will be able to enquire on your Euro accounts and make payments from them through the bank's electronic cash management products such as Password and Keybank.

EMU ON 1 JANUARY 2002 (LATEST)
Euro notes and coins will replace Irish Punt notes and coins from 1 January, 2002 (latest). Implications for your routine banking and payments business from 1 January 2002 with banks are:

- Any of your bank accounts which remain expressed in Irish Punts or in other participating currencies will be converted to Euro free of charge
- You will be obliged by law to express all payment transactions after this date in Euros or a non- participating currency
- Your branch will continue to accept payments (eg cheques) drawn prior to 1 January, 2002 but not lodged/processed prior to that date

IMPLICATIONS FOR INTERNATIONAL COMMERCIAL PAYMENTS
Background
When EMU commences on 1 January 1999 the Euro will become

the official currency of all participating countries. From that date:

- Businesses will be free to trade in Euros although existing nation al currencies can continue to be used in financial transactions until the end of the EMU Transition Period
- Conversion rates (expressed to 6 significant digits) between the Euro and participating national currencies will be irrevocably fixed by the European Union Council. These will be based on fixed exchange rates between participating currencies to be announced around the same time as the initial EMU countries are agreed — probably in May or June, 1998
- The Euro will replace the ECU on a one-for-one basis
- The Euro will be quoted on Foreign Exchange Markets against all non-participating currencies, both those within the EU (including Sterling) and those outside (eg. US Dollars, Japanese Yen.)

EMU Transition Period

Euro notes and coin will be introduced not later than 1 January 2002. The period between 1 January 1999 and the introduction of Euro notes and coins is referred to as the EMU Transition Period. After the introduction of Euro notes and coins it will no longer be possible to transact business in the currencies of participating states — they will have been replaced by the Euro.

However, during the Transition Period, international commercial payments between countries participating in EMU can be settled in national currencies, in Euros or in third country currencies (eg US Dollars, Sterling, Japanese Yen).

Financial instruments such as drafts, cheques, telegraphic transfers, documentary collections and letters of credit will be available from banks in Euros as well as in the wide range of other potential settlement currencies.

Reduced Exchange Risk

The fixing of exchange rates for 1 January 1999 will eliminate the exchange rate risk associated with transactions between countries participating in EMU. Irish importers and exporters will no longer incur the cost of hedging such risks.

International Payments during the EMU transition period
Telegraphic Transfers
Many international trade payments are settled by electronic means — generally referred to as telegraphic transfers. You will be able to make, or receive such payments in Euros from 1 January 1999 and to lodge the proceeds to, or fund the payment from, your bank account whether that is expressed in Irish Punts, in Euros or in another currency.

With the advent of EMU it is likely that a number of new options for processing such payments will emerge by 1 January 1999 or subsequently. This will enable you to choose the most cost-effective options to suit your business requirements. Banks will be able to advise you on the options available and the costs/timescales associated with them.

'Target' — A new European Payment Option
One of the new emerging international payment options is 'Target' which is being developed by the European Monetary Institute (forerunner of the European Central Bank) and the central banks in all EU member states. Its prime objective is to provide an efficient and secure settlement process to facilitate the operation of a single monetary policy across the Euro area. It will, however, also be available for commercial transactions and will offer advantages in efficiency, security and speed of settlement. Although the pricing arrangements for this system have not yet been finalised it is likely to be priced at a somewhat higher level than alternative options.

Euro Drafts
In addition to the current range of foreign currency drafts, banks will be able to provide you with drafts denominated in Euros and drawn on Banks in participating countries from 1 January 1999.

Should you receive payments by way of drafts denominated in Euros and drawn on banks in participating countries, banks will be able to credit your account even if that continues to be denominated in Irish Punts or another currency.

Euro Cheques
Banks in all participating countries, including Ireland, will be pro-

viding their customers with the facility to draw cheques in Euros from 1 January 1999.

You will be able to lodge cheques denominated in Euros to, or draw cheques denominated in Euros from, your bank account whether it is denominated in Irish Punts or in Euros.

Whereas such cheques could be used to effect payment to a supplier in another participating country no plans to standardise cheque clearing systems in the Euro area have yet emerged. Such cheques will, therefore, be processed in the same way and in the same timescale as an Irish Punt cheque would be processed today. For this reason you may find that suppliers who are reluctant to accept payment by IR£ cheque today will also be reluctant to accept a Euro denominated cheque drawn on an Irish bank after 1 January 1999.

Sterling Payments

While the UK is not expected to participate in EMU from the start UK banks are expected to agree shortly on standards to enable their electronic and paper based clearing systems to process payments denominated in Euros from 1 January 1999 in the same timescale as payments denominated in Sterling are processed at present. Irish importers and exporters trading with the UK should therefore experience no difficulty in making or receiving payments expressed in Euros should they wish to do so after 1 January 1999.

TWO CRUCIAL LEGAL EUROPEAN REGULATIONS

The EU council meeting in Dublin in December 1996 approved the text of two EU regulations designed to establish the legal framework for the introduction of the Euro. Irish courts will be obliged to recognise this framework when enacted.

Legal certainty for business

An EU Regulation based on Article 235 of the Treaty of Rome, which established the European community, is designed to create legal certainty around certain issues necessary to facilitate business preparations for Economic and Monetary Union (EMU.) This regulation has been formally adopted by the EU council and has already entered into force following publication in the official *Journal of the European Communities* on the 19th of June, 1997. It applies to all

EU countries whether they join the Euro area or not. The principle areas covered in this regulation are:

- *Continuity of Contract* The introduction of the Euro will not alter, invalidate or excuse the performance of contracts previously entered into unless it has been otherwise agreed by the parties to particular contracts. As a result of this provision the principle of continuity of contracts and other legal instruments whose performance extends beyond the introduction of the Euro will be recognised in all legal jurisdictions of the European Union and it is likely that jurisdictions outside the European Union will recognise it also.
- *Ecu to Euro* References in contracts to the ECU will be interpreted as references to the Euro at a rate of one Euro to one ECU.
- *Exchange Rates* The irrevocably fixed exchange rates between the Euro and participating national currencies will be expressed to six significant digits and may not be rounded or truncated when making conversions.
- *Rounding* Monetary amounts resulting from conversions to or from the Euro may then be rounded up or down to the nearest Eurocent or the smallest unit of the national currency involved. Amounts equal to exactly half such Eurocent or smallest unit will be rounded up.
- *'1 Euro = x'* Rates will be quoted between the Euro and all other currencies. It will not be permissible to derive and use conversion rates between participating national currencies. Conversions between participating national currencies must be carried our through the Euro; i.e. to convert from Irish Punts to French francs you must first convert from Irish Punts into Euros at the fixed irrevocable Euro/Irish Punt rate to at least three decimal places and then convert the resultant Euro amount into French Francs at the fixed irrevocable Euro/French Franc rate.

Currency issues for business

A second regulation based on Treaty Article 109L (4) will be adopted under the Maastricht Treaty when the initial countries participating in EMU are known. It will enter into direct force on 1 January 1999 and will apply to those EU countries that qualify and join the

Euro area. This regulation makes the following provisions:

- *Currency* The currency of participating member states will be the Euro from 1 January 1999 and one Euro will be divided into 100 Euro cents.
- *Euro v. National Currency* For the transitional period (i.e. from 1 January 1999 and ending on the 31st of December 2001 at the latest) it will be possible to denominate contracts either in Euros or in the national currencies of participating countries.
  References to participating currencies in contracts existing at the end of the transition period will be read as references to Euros at the respective irrevocably fixed exchange rates.
- *Payments* During the transitional period it will be possible for you to make payment either in Euros or in National currencies unless the relevant contract provides otherwise. Financial institutions will credit the accounts of creditors in the denomination in which those accounts are expressed, making any conversions necessary at the relevant irrevocably fixed exchange rates.
- *Notes and coins* Euro bank notes and coin will be introduced at a date (before 1 January, 2002) to be decided when the initial participating countries are determined and the legal tender status of the national notes and coins of those countries will cease not more than six months later — the exact date to be determined by national law. The Maastricht Treaty requires that Central Banks will continue to exchange national notes and coin for Euros at the fixed conversion rate after they have ceased to be legal tender.

It is important that you consider whether the effect of these two EU regulations will have implications for your business contracts.

IT SYSTEM CHANGES NEEDED FOR EMU
Changes needed in IT systems will include those arising from:

- Changes in the specification or composition of products introduced to respond to anticipated market developments post EMU (eg pricing and costing systems may have to be adapted to standards used in new markets, by new competition, or to accommodate revised price 'points')

- The need to receive and/or produce payments and financial information in Euro, as well as in Irish Punts or other participating currencies, during the period 1 January 1999 and the 31st of December, 2001.
- The need to continue to communicate with other external or internal systems which may not be adapted for EMU at the same time. Such other external systems may include those of customers, suppliers, bankers, public authorities, etc.
- The ultimate need to switch over all IT systems and databases containing financial information to the Euro completely from 1 January, 2002 including historic information needed for the continued, effective management of the business.
- The need to plan for, and manage, the rounding differences which will inevitably occur in conversions between the Euro and national currencies. The fixed Euro conversion rates will be announced on 1 January 1999 and will contain six significant digits (i.e. the Irish Punt conversion rate will be expressed as 1 Euro = IR£0.xxxxxx.) These rates must be used in converting national currency values into Euros. They may not be rounded or truncated and the use of 'inverse' rates (i.e. rates expressed in the form IR£1 = Euro1.xxxxx) is specifically prohibited.
- The need to convert to Euro any parameters or threshold values used by IT systems in processing which are presently expressed in Irish Punts or other participating currencies.
- The need to adapt systems to print the Euro code ('EUR') and/or Euro symbol () where appropriate (eg on printed cheques, invoices, statements etc)
- The possible need to adapt certain IT system outputs to display both Euro and Irish Punt (or other participating currency) values from 1 January 1999. While no legal obligation in this respect has yet emerged businesses may wish to do this from an early stage as a service to customers.

LIKELY SECTORAL IMPACTS

Retail

As a retailer, you are likely to face heavy up front preparation/conversion costs. The particular issues which arise for this sector include:

- Planning for the processing of non-cash Euro payments during the transitional period and the changeover of the point of sale equipment (including card terminals, cash registers etc.) from 1 January, 2002.

- Planning for the handling of two sets of notes and coins for a period after the Euro notes and coins are introduced. You may need to operate separate tills for Euros and Irish Punts and it will be in the interests of both banks and retailers to co-operate to ensure that the period of dual currency circulation is kept to a minimum. For your part, you may find it helpful to return change in Euros as much as possible.

- Planning for the modification of vending machines to the new notes and coins, as necessary, and deciding whether or not to do this on a 'Big Bang' basis, or on a gradual basis while the two sets of notes/coins circulate.

- Planning for the implications of dual price labelling and the adaptation of bar coding systems for retail products. Where prices are expressed in relation to another variable, such as by weight, you may find it difficult to achieve uncomplicated dual pricing

- Be particularly conscious of the need to create new 'psychological' price points in Euros and of any product changes that this may require. It may have implications for your margins.

- Training of retail staff, particularly point-of-sale staff, will be of major importance to ensure that the changeover period is man aged as efficiently as possible.

Small Cash Based Retailers

If you are a relatively small cash-based retailer, such a s a newsagent or hardware store, the impact of EMU is likely to be large during the transitional period. You may be asked to take payments in Euros, whether by cheque, credit card or other non-cash means. Some suppliers may ask you to pay them in Euros. Therefore, you will need to be aware of the fixed conversion rates, to make sure that your bankers are in a position to accept Euro payments in your lodgements, and that you also have the means to make Euro payments.

Agriculture

From January, 1999 CAP payments will be expressed in Euros and the Green Pound system will be redundant. This will lead to greater price stability/transparency and hopefully greater cohesion by eliminating the demands for European and national subsidies currently arising from Green Pound revaluation. In general, as a farmer you can expect to benefit from the anticipated lower interest rates and inflation rates, but you will still be exposed to:

- Risks associated with the potential volatility in exchange rates leading up to 1999
- The rate at which the IR£ is locked into other participating currencies
- UK exchange rate policy after 1999 for as long as Sterling remains outside the Euro area

You may also benefit in the longer term from general growth in economic activity stimulated by EMU, and may be able to source supplies more competitively as a result of the wider Euro market. Overall, it is important to recognise, however, that the evolution of the World Trade Organisation, and the enlargement plans for the European Union, will have more significant long-term implications for agriculture than EMU.

Manufacturing

The impact of EMU on manufacturers will depend on the exact nature of your business, its financial structure, the sector in which it operates, and where your existing and potential customers are. Clearly, if you have significant borrowings you will benefit from the expected lower Irish interest rates. If a substantial proportion of your output is exported to the UK you will remain exposed to potential Sterling devaluation for as long as it stays outside EMU. If your output is primarily destined for non-EU markets, on the other hand, EMU is likely to have a limited affect on your competitive position.

In common with every other business, you will also have to plan the conversion of accounting, financial and management information systems and procedures and decide on the timing of such conversions. EMU may not require significant changes in your manufacturing processes, other than where a need arises to adapt products to the size, quality or other standards suited for new market environments or for new 'psychological' price points. In the longer term however, price transparency across the Euro area will present both opportunities and threats for manufacturing businesses. Opportunities may enable you to penetrate a new wider market, whether on a niche or mass market basis. Threats will be encountered in the form of new players encouraged to enter your existing markets because of the elimination of exchange rate exposure and possibly because of opportunities arising for them from increased transparency of pricing. EMU will increase the pressure on you to be efficient.

Export/Import Businesses

If you are engaged in trading activities with the countries participating in EMU you will benefit immediately from the elimination of exchange risk, because you will no longer need to hedge such risk which incurs risk premium in payment transaction costs. Furthermore, greater price transparency across the Euro area can be expected to increase competition in export markets. If you are an importer, you may be able to source supplies more competitively.

Tourism

The tourist industry should be a key beneficiary of EMU because the elimination of exchange risk will make it easier to price and sell Irish holidays in other participating countries. Tourist operators such as hotels, restaurants etc., will also gain from reduced costs and effort in handling payments from tourists from other participating countries. On the other hand, the tourist industry will remain exposed to potential Sterling devaluation for as long as the UK stays outside EMU.

Financial Sector

In the short term, at least, the financial sector will be more adversely effected by EMU than any other sector. In addition to losing substantial revenue from foreign exchange and Irish Punt currency trading, banks will incur heavy costs in preparing systems and operating procedures. In the medium to long term, however, monetary union is expected to generate increased economic activity, which should provide some compensation for the upfront loses it will incur.

Trade between Punt and Sterling Areas

If you are involved with cross border trade between the Irish Punt and Sterling areas, including Northern Ireland, you will be particularly affected by EMU if IR£ joins and Sterling remains outside.

Not alone will such trade will be particularly exposed to any deterioration in the value of Sterling against the Euro, but conversions between IR£ and Sterling will become more complicated from the beginning of 1999 when the relevant official exchange rates will be based on conversions via the Euro.

It is unlikely, therefore, that a cross rate between IR£ and Stg£ will be quoted by 'official' sources. For transactions involving large sums it will be important to take into account the official Euro rates when giving or accepting price quotations. For smaller retail type transactions it is probable that sellers will quote and do business on, indicative rates between IR£ and Stg£.

You should also be aware that, even though Sterling will not be an early participant in the Euro, some businesses in the Sterling area may wish to invoice and/or be invoiced in Euros from the beginning of the next year or soon thereafter.

CHAPTER 8

Personal Financial Matters in Ireland

Ireland is a modern, economically sophisticated country and as such operates the full panoply of taxes so beloved of modern governments, the most significant of these and the ones most likely to be encountered by the average tax payer include:

- Income Tax (with a range of Allowances)
- Pay Related Social Insurance (social security contributions)
- Capital Acquisitions Tax (embracing Gift Tax and Inheritance Tax)
- Corporation Tax (with a range of Capital Allowances)
- Capital Gains Tax
- Value Added Tax

Emphasising that this book is not intended as a tax planner, but rather a guide to some basic principles and operating procedures, we nevertheless outline the fundamentals of Income Tax, Pay Related Social Insurance and touch on the standard rates of Value Added Tax since these are the most commonly encountered taxes of everyday life. If your personal financial situation is more complicated or such that you will be involved with any of the other taxes, or simply that you need to know more about the many tax reliefs and allowances available, then you should seek professional advice from an accountant or financial advisor well versed in these specific areas.

If alternatively you enjoy sorting out your own affairs or want to acquire greater personal understanding, then a good starting point would be to obtain a copy of *Tolley's Taxation in the Republic of Ireland* which is published regularly in order to keep abreast of changing legislation and case law.

Be aware that should you fall foul of the authorities or fail to comply fully with the requirements of the system with regard to disclosing all of your financial affairs there is a comprehensive collection of anti-avoidance legislation with commensurate penalties. You have been warned! If disputes arise then there is also a formal appeals procedure.

All of the taxes mentioned above are ultimately administered by the Revenue Commissioners. Although they can offer some advice on general principles, operating procedures and current practice, they are not, as they say themselves 'a vehicle for debate on arguable issues, advance rulings or assistance in relation to tax planning'.

For information on all taxes excluding Value Added Tax contact:
The Revenue Commissioners
Dublin Castle
Dublin 2

For information on Value Added Tax regulations contact:
The Revenue Commissioners (VAT)
Castle House
South Great George's Street
Dublin 2

For queries on returns and payments of Value Added Tax:
The Collector-General
Apollo House
Tara Street
Dublin 2

Price Waterhouse publish some useful guides, particularly *The Pocket Tax Guide* and *Foreign Citizens Working in the Republic of Ireland.*

International Assignment Service
Price Waterhouse
Gardner House
Wilton Place
Dublin 2
Tel: (01) 662 6000 / Fax: (01) 662 6615

THE FUNDAMENTALS

- The tax year runs from 6 April to 5 April, familiar to United Kingdom taxpayers if no one else!

- Budget day is normally in December, so December 1997's budget covered the tax year commencing 6 April 1998, with most significant fiscal and taxation changes coming into effect from that date, but with some welfare changes occurring in June and very often duties on petrol, tobacco and alcohol taking immediate effect to avoid stockpiling!

- The Irish version of the modern state's social security or insurance levy is 'Pay Related Social Insurance' which is paid by the great majority of employees and self-employed persons as well as their employers. Like most of these levies they are intended to fund a variety of welfare and retirement benefits.
  For instance, in 1997/98, employers paid 8.5 percent of an employee's pay if it did not exceed £260 per week. For employees earning more than £260 per week the employer had to find 12 percent to a maximum employee earnings' ceiling of £536 per week. Employees made no contribution if they earned less than £80 per week, but paid 4.5 percent on earnings between £80 and £446 per week.

- Income tax is usually collected through 'Pay As You Earn', being deducted at source by the employer. Taking the current tax year 1998/99 as our example, the rates of income tax were 26 percent on the first £9,900 of a single person's taxable earnings — or £19,800 of a married couple's — and 48 percent on taxable earnings above these levels. To alleviate these levels there are the usual tax allowances for particular needs, such as allowances for single people of £4,000, £8,000 for a married couple, £2,900 for single parents, £450 for each of the first two children and £650 thereafter, etc.

- As a new employee starting work in Ireland you will need to obtain a Tax Free Allowance Certificate which will probably mean filling in a Form 12A. Speak to your employer or local Revenue Commissioners' Office. If you do not have a valid certificate then the employer is obliged to apply increasingly penal rates of tax on your pay, starting at 26 percent of all your earnings and rising to a hefty 48 percent of your income from your ninth week of earning.

- You can obtain limited tax relief on your mortgage interest payments, but these are fairly modest and have been reducing over recent times. You can also obtain tax relief on rent paid for private rented accommodation.
- Contributions by an employee to an occupational pension scheme are given relief from both Income Tax and Pay Related Social Insurance.
- For the self-employed the system is somewhat different. Though the levels of tax and allowances are the same, there are special rules concerning allowable business expenses. As a self-employed person you will have to make a lump sum payment before 1 November each year and then provide a detailed tax return by the end of the following January, at which point any under- or over-payments of tax will be resolved.

We can only emphasise again that you should seek professional advice regarding your own particular tax affairs, as there are a host of other complexities and allowances which may well apply to you.

As a final piece of information we attach here a table showing the comparative take-home pay for a number of different earners. The figures were compiled by Price Waterhouse using October 1997 exchange rates and assume the deduction of Federal Income Tax, Social Security, New York State and Ontario Provincial Tax.

AFTER TAX SALARY COMPARISON IN PUNTS

	Married Couple, 2 Children			Child	Single Person
Gross Salary	£20,000	£35,000	£50,000	Benefit	£35,000
Ireland	15,353	24,015	31,444	720	20,445
UK	15,162	25,770	34,770	1,158	25,464
USA	16,579	26,866	35,945	none	23,172
Canada	14,877	23,455	30,678	1,017	22,636
France	15,560	26,382	36,438	921	22,780
Germany	15,022	23,228	32,704	1,956	19,899

Bald income figures only tell half the story, since the cost of living can vary markedly from country to country, making a seemingly generous level of income shrink alarmingly when confronted by high living costs. Thus a table for comparison reasons is now included with all the usual caveats regarding lifestyle assumptions, exchange rates, the fact that Dublin is generally agreed to be more expensive than elsewhere in the country, etc.

PRICE COMPARISON: DUBLIN MEAN PRICES = 100

Index Category	Frankfurt	New York	Paris	London
Food at Home	105	116	102	108
Alcohol and Tobacco	60	74	63	97
Domestic Supplies	97	93	99	104
Personal Care	96	99	109	111
Clothing and Footwear	94	97	100	102
Home Services	130	143	137	120
Utilities	91	118	114	104
Entertainment	103	103	118	118
Transportation	83	69	88	105
TOTAL	96	98	102	107
Excluding Utilities	97	97	101	97
Excluding Transportation	99	104	105	107

VALUE ADDED TAX

In common with all European Union states Ireland operates Value Added Tax. As a business you must register for VAT purposes if your turnover exceeds £20,000 per annum as a service supplier, or £40,000 as a supplier of goods. The standard rate of VAT is 21 percent, with a number of exceptions:

- A reduced rate of 12.5 percent is charged on newspapers, restaurants, cinema tickets, heating fuel and electricity
- VAT is not paid on exports, books, food, children's clothing and footwear, education and training, theatre tickets, insurance and banking services and passenger transport

VEHICLE REGISTRATION TAX (VRT)

In addition to VAT at 21 percent there is a special tax on the first registration of new or second-hand vehicles. In 1997 this was levied at a rate of 23.2 percent on vehicles with engine capacities up to 2,500cc and 29.25 percent on those with engine capacities above this level. If applicable, VRT must be paid within one working day of the vehicle's importation.

WILLS

Every adult should make a will. In Ireland, if you die intestate — that is, without a will — then the provisions of the 1965 Succession Act take effect:

- If you leave a spouse, but no children, the spouse will inherit your whole estate
- If you leave a spouse and children, the spouse inherits two thirds and the children one third between them
- If you leave children, but no spouse, they inherit the entire estate divided equally between them
- If you leave no relatives at all then the state will ultimately take possession of all your whole estate

To be valid in law a will must be signed by yourself and witnessed by someone who will neither themselves nor their spouse become beneficiaries. It is important that your will actually achieves what you intended and it makes sense to have it drawn up properly by a solicitor. The normal, straightforward will should not cost a great deal, but ask for an estimate of the fee first if in any doubt.

There are various taxes payable on the estates of deceased persons. In crude terms, beneficiaries other than a spouse may have to pay Capital Acquisition Tax. In 1997/98 the children and parents of a deceased person could receive £185,550 each before becoming liable to tax.

Probate Tax is also payable — but not by a spouse — at a rate of 2 percent on the net assets of your estate if they exceed £10,820 after meeting funeral costs. Upon divorce, a spouse loses succession rights. However, the estates of deceased persons, and all the tax planning that is possible, is an absolute minefield for the unwary — which takes in 99 percent of us — so seek professional, expert advice.

CHAPTER 9

House Buying and Moving

HOUSE BUYING

Almost certainly the most important decisions you will have to make are about the size, style and location of your new home. This is not really a matter of money — though the higher your spending power the wider your choices will be — but rather of the kind of life that you wish to live. Do you need to be near to work or a communications hub? Do you want to be close to some particular interest or leisure pursuit? Do you have children who will need to go to a particular school? Do you need lots of extra space to accommodate family or hobby? Do you dream of a Georgian town house, a rambling country cottage, a smart, new, modern house with plenty of labour-saving fittings and fixtures?

There is no doubt about it, this is a crucial decision: the wrong one will invariably lead to discontent and frustration. Do not rush into the decision: make sure that you weigh up all the pros and cons, because you will have to live *in* the result. An error will undoubtedly make your move to Ireland unsatisfactory.

The amount you can afford will obviously shape your initial thinking. Given the way that house prices have spiralled in Ireland over the past decade, deciding how much you can realistically afford is therefore a significant decision. Up until even six years ago people rarely spoke about property prices and you could still buy, if you were in the right place at the right time, an old farmhouse 'down the country' with an acre or two for as little as £15,000 (though in truth it probably needed considerable rebuilding!).

Today conversations buzz with the latest property prices. In Ireland, the property boom — not quite on the scale of south-eastern England in the late eighties, but not far behind in certain desirable areas — coincided with the economic and jobs boom, and by Irish standards the increases have been substantial and unprecedented.

As well as people from many other countries, the Dutch and Germans have been particularly active in buying second homes in Ireland and the age-old rule of 'supply and demand' controls the house prices. With such a buoyant economic environment people have been purchasing houses as investments and for commercial letting as well as family bolt-holes pending a more permanent move.

The Irish government has been very concerned about rapidly rising house-price inflation and is closely monitoring it. It is even rumoured to have considered some form of legislation to control, or at least check, the fast rising prices. Ireland's adoption of the Euro in 1999 is also causing some concern as it is widely expected (though not yet known for sure — so no lawsuits if this proves false!) that the Europe-wide interest rate will be set at a level that is below that currently set by the Irish Central Bank, thus pouring yet more fuel on an already highly volatile situation.

As you might expect from a country that was ruled from London for many centuries, the Irish have adopted a legal procedure for purchasing property that is very similar to that of England and Wales, but not Scotland. As in England you should be able to complete the deal within eight weeks of signing a contract, though every deal is naturally subject to its own peculiar factors that can speed or slow this timescale.

BUYING AT AUCTION

One of the main differences between buying property in Ireland and the UK, is that in Ireland, nearly all properties and land are sold through auctioneers as opposed to estate agents. A property is advertised, in the local or national press, with the guide price it is expected to fetch and details of the time and place of the auction. You can, however, make an offer through the auctioneer prior to the auction. If your offer is accepted you pay a small deposit, (normally 10 percent), and the property is technically yours; it will be withdrawn from auction. On the other hand, you may decide to experience the excitement of attending the auction in person on the day and join the bidding. If successful, you will have to pay a deposit, again normally about 10 percent, on the day (and the balance within a very short period of time) and be able to leave the auction knowing that the property is yours.

Many of the auctioneers have the facilities to allow you to make an offer and do all your dealings from the UK and even bid by telephone on the day of the auction itself. (Having, we hope, seen the property in question!)

Be cautious, as in any auction, it is important to know what you can afford, decide what is the highest, realistic price that you can go to and stick to it! Do not allow the atmosphere to overwhelm your common sense and good judgement.

Irish Auctioneers and Valuers Institute
38 Merrion Square
Dublin 2
Tel: (01) 661 1794

PROPERTY PRICE TRENDS

Of course, the annual inflation rate statistics only tell part of the story, and the quite extraordinary rate of property price increases should not be forgotten. The national average price increase was around 20 percent in 1996 and was predicted to top 20 percent in 1997; new house prices rose by around 17 percent in the first half of 1997 alone to reach £78,000, with previously owned house prices rising less fast, but still reaching an average of £77,000 during the same period.

The Irish share a passion for home-ownership with their British neighbours, there being over a million home-owners in a population of little more than three and a half million people. High interest rates have done little to diminish this passion. The rise in prices has been general across Ireland, but is driven by different mixes of factors that result in marked variations.

As the capital and main business centre, Dublin has enjoyed (or suffered?) the greatest general rate of increase, fuelled by an influx of foreign business people, returning Irish and the rapidly rising level of economic activity. During the first half of 1997 new home prices rose by 25 percent to an average £94,000, with used home prices rising at a similar rate of 20 percent to reach £97,000.

Some smaller communities around Dublin have seen dramatic price increases — especially when a major industrial concern sets up nearby — often seeing a typical three-bedroom semi-detached house almost doubling in price since 1991 to around £75,000.

Other major urban centres such as Cork and particularly Galway have experienced slightly more modest price rises on the back of the economic upsurge; in Galway prices have risen by about 10 percent in the first half of 1997 to see new homes average £86,000 and used homes £77,000 whilst in Cork the figures reached £76,000 for a new house and £67,000 for a second-hand one, whilst comparable prices in Limerick reached £69,000 and £61,000.

The demand for rural dwellings, from humble cottages to grander estates has also seen considerable growth. This interest is particularly powered by 'in-comers' looking for a quiet life and the chance to enjoy Ireland's unique charm or the opportunity to set up in business using the space and outbuildings of a large property for development purposes.

This does not mean that bargains are not to be had, but it is true that the Irish themselves are now well aware of the value of their assets and any investor should bear in mind that the happy-go-lucky image of the Irish belies a shrewd and canny ability to bargain and drive a hard deal!

Remember, too, that the auction-based house sale process in Ireland has been seen as helping to fuel some of the more speculative increases, but it is hoped that new rules introduced in 1997 by the Institute of Irish Auctioneers and Valuers regarding the setting and publishing of guide prices should remove some of the more inflationary sales.

MORTGAGES

Borrowing money for house purchases is very similar to UK practice, ie very broadly 20 or 25-year terms, 2.5 salary multipliers, a mortgage arrangement fee usually around 0.5 percent of the mortgage amount and a maximum amount of money lent equating to 90 percent of the house price — though of course your personal circumstances could lead to any number of variations from these norms. The now familiar choice of fixed or variable rate, repayment or endowment mortgages are available as well as specialist ones such as pension mortgages for the self-employed. Seek independent financial advice if you are not sure which best meets your needs.

It has generally been thought unduly risky for most people to borrow in one currency whilst earning an income in another. This is because you are at the mercy of two national economies, two interest rates and the associated exchange rate movements. For instance, in the 1980s there was a vogue in Britain to borrow money in Deutschmarks because the German interest rate was then below, by a wide margin, those prevailing in the UK. Unfortunately, when Sterling weakened against the Deutschmark, people had to find more and more pounds to buy the same amount of Deutschmarks to meet their repayments. As German interest rates also crept up, the double jeopardy became too much for some of the borrowers to cope with financially.

As the United Kingdom is not, for the moment, joining those European countries adopting the Euro as their currency, there still remains the possibility of taking out a mortgage from a European source, in a currency other than Sterling. Do so only after good advice and with a great deal of care!

To eliminate currency fluctuation and risk, so far as repayments are concerned, the Bank of Ireland has introduced a Sterling-denominated mortgage specifically for the purchase of properties in Ireland; that is, you borrow and repay in Sterling, having bought a Punt/Euro valued asset. The normal criteria for assessing the granting of a mortgage apply, but it is an interesting example of a flexible financial product created to meet a market need.

TAXATION AND FEES

These are an important elements of cost in house purchasing although easily overlooked. You must take them into consideration alongside all the other expenses.

Purchase Deed Stamp Duty

This is chargeable on all transactions involving used houses and on new houses that exceed an area of 125sq m (1,346sq ft). The rules for calculating the duty on new houses can be complex, so check with the developer. For used houses the following scale applies (the appropriate percentage applies to the full purchase price):

Purchase Price	Stamp Duty
to £5,000	nil
£5,001 to £10,000	1%
£10,001 to 15,000	2%
£15,001 to 25,000	3%
£25,001 to £50,000	4%
£50,001 to £60,000	5%
£60,001 to £150,000	6%
£150,001 to £160,000	7%
£160,001 to £170,000	8%
£170,001 plus	9%

Mortgage Stamp Duty

This is levied at a rate of 0.1 percent on all mortgages over £20,000 to a maximum of £500.

Legal Fees

The Incorporated Law Society of Ireland can provide both a list of solicitors in the area you wish to move into, as well as guidelines on the fees you can expect to pay. Using a solicitor is sensible, especially for an overseas buyer, as you will inevitably be unfamiliar with the intricacies of the local system and practice.

Furthermore it is a sensible precaution to have some inspection made of local and regional development plans for things such as new house or factory construction, new roads, electricity pylons, sewerage plants, etc.

The Law Society of Ireland
Blckhall Place
Dublin 7
Tel: (o1) 671 0711

Valuation Fees

As in the UK, lenders require a third party valuation of the property under question. This should be done by a surveyor to check that the house is not being unduly inflated in value, ie that the lender will be able to dispose of it should it need to and raise enough money to pay of the borrowing.

Structural Survey

It is always worth having this done by a reputable surveyor, not least for your own comfort, but also because the lender will require it in order to assess the condition of the property's physical fabric.

Architects and Surveyors Institute
7 Woodbine Park
Blackrock
Dublin
Tel: (01) 269 4462

Registration of Title

Your solicitor will handle this and advise on costs.

SOCIAL HOUSING

There is social housing in Ireland as well as Local Authority House Purchase Loans and Local Authority House Improvement Loans. Housing is allocated on the basis of a points system with more points given for a greater need. The loan schemes are aimed at low income earners. In either case it has to be said that as the supplies are limited it is unlikely that someone arriving new in a local area would be given particularly high priority.

Irish Council for Social Housing
50 Merrion Square
East Dublin 2
Tel: (01) 661 8335

FIRST TIME BUYER GRANTS

If you are a first time buyer, you may qualify for a first-time buyer's grant of £3,000. You must fulfil certain criteria, such as the obvious ones:

- You are a first time buyer
- The property is a new construction
- It will be your primary place of residence
- It must have a floor area of between 35sq m and 125sq m
  j109
(376sq ft to 1,345 sq ft).

If you think you may be eligible for or wish to register for this grant, contact:

Department of the Environment
Housing Grants Section
Government Offices
Ballina
County Mayo
Tel: (096) 70677

LOCAL SERVICE CHARGES
With the abolition of water rates, as of January 1997 the only local charges levied are for refuse collection. These vary depending on location, but should be in the region of £100 per annum.

PLANNING AND BUILDING REGULATIONS
Ireland does have building and planning regulations and, as in the United Kingdom, you should either contact your local government authority before commencing any construction or alteration, or at the very least ensure that your builder, contractor, surveyor or architect has notified the correct parties and has received the proper authorisations and permits.

Royal Institute of the Architects of Ireland
8 Merrion Square
North Dublin 2
Tel: (01) 676 1703

MOVING
Having found the home of your dreams and successfully completed the purchase, you have done the easy bit! You now have the hard work of actually moving yourself, your family and possessions overseas. Moving is a very stressful operation, traditionally up there with marriage, divorce and bereavement, but yet has its own reward — the sense of changing for the better: new beginnings and fresh starts. To move abroad may seem even more daunting, but do not despair. With just a little research, planning and forethought everything can be arranged relatively simply.

To begin with, there are many firms of removers who specialise in moving your valued furniture and personal belongings to overseas destinations, including Ireland, both quickly and safely. If possible use a firm that has been recommended to you. If none has, choose one that is a member of the British Association of Removers, North American International or similar trade body that tries to enforce standards of contract and behaviour as this should mean that you are dealing with a reputable business that values its good name and reputation.

As further protection you could consider opting for a removal company that operates the Advance Payments Guarantee Scheme. This scheme is only offered through participating members of the Overseas Group of the British Association of Removers. Companies have to opt in, so it is not automatically available. The purpose of the scheme is to ensure that, in the event of your removal firm — to whom you have entrusted your possessions and to whom you have made an up-front payment — collapsing, your property will be delivered to its contracted destination at no further cost.

British Association of Removers
3 Churchill Court
58 Station Road
North Harrow HA2 7SA
Tel: (0181) 861 3331
Fax: (0181) 861 3332

Always get the details of your move (timing and dates, price, route, any special arrangements regarding fragile or valuable items, loading/unloading, storage, shipping, the remover's terms and conditions) confirmed in writing. Always check the insurance cover and make sure that the amount is sufficient to cover your possessions fully.

The cost of every move is different as it depends on the mix of the above features, the size, weight and quantity of items concerned, as well as the distance and difficulty involved in physically getting from your old to your new home. It is highly recommended that a representative of the company visits you at your current home to inspect the nature of the items you intend moving, to answer any questions and note any special requests you may have.

Some Relocation Companies

Celtic Relocations
Fastnet
Castleknock
Carrigaline
County Cork
Tel: (021) 373 763
Fax: (021) 373 386

PHH Ireland
Merchants House
27-30 Merchants Quay
Dublin 8
Tel: (01) 671 0022
Fax: (01) 671 0712

Corporate Care
27 Linden Avenue
Beaumont
Cork
Tel: (021) 294 878

Relocation Services International Ltd
Clareville
Streamstown
Malahide
County Dublin
Tel/Fax: (01) 490 3902

A & A Cronin Movers (Ireland) Ltd
Security House
66 Baldoyle
Industrial Estate
Dublin 13
Tel: (01) 839 1261
Fax: (01) 839 0140

POSSESSIONS

Generally, if you are moving to Ireland from any member state of the European Community, you are allowed to bring with you without any tax impositions any possessions that you can prove you owned before making your move. Regulations regarding the import of motor cars are slightly tougher, in that you have to be able to provide evidence that you have been driving the vehicle for at least six months before your move.

There is a 'window' during which you can physically bring in your belongings, this being a period of one year before, to one year after, you take up residence. Once legally in the country you may dispose of your possessions as you wish.

For people moving from countries outside the European Community different rules apply! To bring with you your possessions without any tax implications you must be able to show that you owned and were using the items for at least six months before your move. The 'window' extends between six months before and one year after your date of residence, and you cannot dispose of such goods within the first year from that point.

MOTOR VEHICLES

It is important to comply with the regulations concerning vehicles because you could be heavily fined if the rules are not followed.

Vehicles are subject to both Value Added Tax at 21 percent and Vehicle Registration Tax of either 23.2 percent or 29.25 percent (1997 figures) depending on the engine capacity. You may, however, be exempt from these imposts if you are moving from within the European Community and can prove that you purchased the vehicle privately and paid Value Added Tax on it at that time. Contact your local Vehicle Registration Office or:

Office of the Revenue Commissioners
Dublin Castle
Dublin 2 Tel: (01) 679 2777

PETS

United Kingdom quarantine regulations are especially (some think notoriously) severe and Irish regulations are similarly tough. The advantage is that pets can be freely moved directly between Britain, the Isle of Man, and the Channel Islands (provided that the animal in question has been there for at least six months) and Ireland without quarantine restrictions.

Animals — the normal run of cats and dogs — from countries other than the United Kingdom, whether European Union members or not, will be required to spend six months in an approved establishment. Exotic and endangered species may require special permissions and you should be sure to enquire first.

You should ideally approach the Department of Agriculture at least four months before your intended trip in order to arrange housing for your animals and the necessary import licences.

The fee for the six-month period of accommodation for any cat is £1,000. For a dog it is approximately £1,200, but will vary according to the animal's size.

There is currently a good deal of discussion concerning the possibility of changing Ireland's quarantine regulations, especially concerning pets from other European Union member states, so check with your local Irish Embassy or Consulate as to the very latest legal requirements.

Restricted Dogs

Following a series of well publicised attacks, particularly on children, by certain breeds of dogs, Ireland now places restrictions on the following strains and crosses. They must be firmly controlled at all times in public places, which means they must be held on a leash by someone aged at least 17, they must be muzzled and they must wear a collar giving the owner's name and address. Penalties for not observing these regulations include severe fines, seizure of the animal or both. The animals concerned are:

American Pit Bull Terrier
English Bull Terrier
Ban Dog
Bull Dog
Bull Mastiff
Doberman Pinscher
German Shepherd

Japanese Akita
Japanese Tosa
Rhodesian Ridgeback
Rottweiler
Staffordshire Bull Terrier

If you have any questions about quarantine or any matter relating to the bringing animals into the Republic, contact:

Quarantine Section
Department of Agriculture
Lissenhall Kennels
Swords County
Dublin
Tel: (01) 840 1776

Veterinary Division
Department of Agriculture
Kildare Street
Dublin 2
Tel: (01)

UTILITIES AND TRADES

It need hardly be stated that you will need to have your newly acquired home connected to the various utilities and services that are so essential to modern life. You may also need to hire decorators and builders to improve or extend the property or just to make it ship-shape.

Builders and Decorators

We have all heard the exposés of the less reputable members of the building and decorating trades. It is a shame that what is undoubtedly a small, rogue element has so tarnished the reputation of an entire industry when the great majority of practitioners deliver a good quality of service. It is probably because we are so emotionally attached to our homes that we feel in some way violated and react so strongly when a stranger rips into it leaving a trail of disaster behind.

Dealing with members of the building and decorating trades is no different in Ireland than it is in the UK — or anywhere in the world! This means that, ideally, you should use firms that have been recommended to you or whose work you have been able to inspect for yourself. We also recommend that, for the larger projects in particular, it is always advisable to use tradesmen belonging to one of the various trade associations, as this does show some commitment to meeting a certain standard of work.

The costs of trades and builders vary from region to region, but as a general rule they are comparable to those in the UK. To reduce the likelihood of problems here a few simple rules:

- When you require building work it is good practice to get at least three quotes for reasons of comparison and cost assessment.
- Always obtain written quotes with sufficient detail of time, materials and labour involved, so as to be able to make comparisons.
- Get and keep receipts for any deposits or advances you make.
- Check that all local planning department rules and regulations have been complied with and permissions granted before work starts.
- Check that all local planning department rules and regulations are complied with and permissions granted during the work: eg that the site and the work are inspected when they need to be. Redigging foundations to show an inspector they are deep enough can prove costly in time and money.

In some parts of Ireland various voluntary organisations provide a free home draughtproofing and insulation service for pensioners living alone. Contact:

Energy Action
20 Lower Dominick Street
Dublin 1
Tel: (01) 872 3737

Electricity Supply
Electricity is available through the national grid in all but the most remote and isolated places, so getting connected should not

normally be a problem. If you are buying a house without a power connection, check that a supply can be brought in and exactly who will pay for bringing the supply to the house.

You will, of course, need to register as the new occupant.

In Ireland domestic electricity runs at 220 volts and Ireland uses the British pattern of three-pin plugs.

Electricity Supply Board (ESB)
Account Enquiries/Connections
Fleet Sreet
Dublin 2
Tel: (01) 677 8855

Association of Electrical Contractors of Ireland
Mckinley House
Main Street
Blackrock
County Dublin
Tel: (01) 288 6499

Gas Supply

The state-run Bord Gais (gas) has access to restricted supplies and only provides connections within a limited zone, essentially the greater Dublin metropolitan area and along the Eastern seaboard. You should check with the Bord as to the availability in your chosen location if your house is not currently connected to the system. As with electricity you will have to let the Bord Gas know of your new house occupation.

Bord Gais
Administration Office
D'Olier Street and Sir John Rogerson's Quay
Dublin 2
Tel: (01) 602 1212 or (01) 671 2422

You will find that bottled gas is quite a popular fuel in many places in Ireland, although for central heating systems you may have to rely on an oil-fuelled system.

Water and Sewerage Services

The Department of Environment, together with local government authorities, administers the supply of water and sewerage services. You are required first to contact your County Council to register your occupancy and any work or connections that need to be undertaken will be dealt with by them. The Department of Environment will normally fund the connection to mains supply if you purchase a property not currently part of the network.

Water Services and Sewerage Enquiries
ENFO (Environmental Information Services)
17 St Andrew Street
Dublin 2
Tel: (01) 679 3144

CHAPTER 10

Employment

Who would have predicted ten years ago that instead of people leaving Ireland to find well paid, regular employment and an improved standard of living, they would be flocking in quite the reverse direction? No doubt many more people would consider moving to Ireland if they had greater confidence in the jobs market. Despite enormous strides in encouraging inward and domestic commercial investment and making the maximum use of European Union grants and subsidies, unemployment is still running at around 12 percent of the workforce. Of course, this figure reveals at least as much as it conceals, given that certain areas of the country suffer chronic, structural unemployment, while other areas are experiencing a boom in available jobs but a considerable shortage of the skills necesssary to perform then. There are many government programmes that recognise the problems experienced by certain areas of the country in reducing this hardcore unemployment. The programmes offer everything from training to subsidised employment and premises, and from start-up grants to tax holidays.

WORK PERMITS

Irish nationals, of course, require no permission to work in Ireland. An Irish national is defined as:

- Someone born in the country
- Someone whose parents were born in the country or, perhaps if
- You can provide evidence, someone with at least one grandparent who was born in the country
- If you are married to someone qualifying under any of the pre-

ceding categories you, too, can work without any special legalities or qualifications.

As part of the European Community, any citizen of another member state and their spouse can also freely seek employment in Ireland, though you do have to register at your local Garda (Police) Station for a residence permit if you intend to stay for a period exceeding three months.

Everyone else will need a work permit. These are issued by the Ministry for Enterprise, Trade and Employment and you will generally have to meet certain basic criteria to qualify:

- Your employer must seek a permit for you before your arrival
- All efforts must have been made to fill any job vacancy by someone who already has the right to employment

Work Permit Section
Department of Enterprise, Reade and Employment
Room 105
Davitt House
Adelaide Road
Dublin 2

Local Employment Service
Special Unit
FAS
27-33 Upper Baggot Street
Dublin 4
Tel: (01) 668 5777

REVENUE AND SOCIAL INSURANCE NUMBER

Whether or not you require a work permit, you will certainly require a Revenue and Social Security number. This number is unique to you within the tax and social welfare systems and is the means by which the taxes you pay are correctly recorded and, more importantly, that social security deductions are logged against your account. This is very important as some welfare entitlements are dependent on the level and history of contributions that you have managed during your working life.

You must complete a Form 12A which you can obtain from your local tax office. An attempt will be made to trace your old number if you have forgotten it or alternatively you will be issued with a new one.

EMPLOYMENT OVERVIEW

With different industries and services generating different levels of demand for different mixes of skills at any given time, it makes good sense to do some homework on the local employment situation before you go or at least plan what you will do immediately you arrive.

The scale of investment from overseas has really been quite staggering considering the size of Ireland's domestic market. This proves a remarkable testament to Ireland's successful exploitation of its young, well-educated workforce, its lifestyle opportunities, excellent, modern telecommunications and good transport links, its use of the English language, carefully targeted tax and investment incentives and its enthusiastic membership of the European Union. It also means that good employment opportunities exist for those with the necessary skills.

Manufacturing

Manufacturing industries were the original targets for Ireland's development agencies, especially those intending to export the majority of their products. Engineering in the automobile and aerospace sectors is well represented with the value of components manufactured in and exported from Ireland to car producers around the world approaching US$1 billion per annum.

Oil and Gas Exploration

Five times as many oil wells will be drilled around the coast of Ireland over the next ten years as there have been in the past ten years. Each one will cost £10 million to drill, of which approximately 40 percent will be spent in Ireland. In hard statistics, this means that there are now 140 wells around the Irish coast, with at least a further five per year projected over the next decade. Each rig costs £150,000 per day to service when drilling, while the three drilling rigs off the west coast this summer were spending in the order of £1 million every two days.

Now the call is going out for top quality Irish companies to join the list of those willing to provide goods and services to this expanding industry. To quote from a recent seminar held in Galway, the centre for this industry in the West of Ireland, 'Oil rigs are like a microcosm of society, they require everything from seabed engineering, marine engineering, environmental engineering, boats and helicopters, labour, communications and electronic systems. It is not beyond the realms of possibility that Irish companies can become suppliers, and if they perform well they will be kept on.'

Suppliers must be members of OSCAR, which is the international registration system for companies supplying the oil industry. Forbairt, which has developed its own oil and gas register for the Irish industry, is available to advise Irish hopefuls on the entrance requirements for OSCAR. Oil companies are then obliged to advertise in the EU journal for any contracts beyond a certain threshold. Forbairt has also developed an Irish goods and services operation, designed to sell the services of Irish companies to the oil industry to provide a technical linkage between the Irish service providers and the oil companies. Forbairt, as the government agency which has had the most lasting involvement in oil exploration in Ireland, is in a position to advise oil companies in this respect.

Electronics

Some 30 percent of all American investment into Europe is going to Ireland, a percentage that reaches 40 percent for American electronics firms. The total number of companies now engaged in all manner of telecommunications, hardware and software development and manufacture exceeds 300 — they constitute a third of all Ireland's exports by value. Something like 60 percent of all business application software sold in Europe each year is manufactured in Ireland, with Microsoft leading the market in localisation and translation services.

The objective for the year 2010 is that 20,000 people will be employed in Dublin's software industry, or an additional net 1,000 jobs per annum, and that the city will become a Top Three location for software in Europe.

Over the past 12 years, Dublin has developed a reputation as Europe's leading centre for the computer software industry. The industry employs about 12,000 people nationally. Reports show that 71 percent of indigenous companies are located in the Dublin region, employing 8,000 people. Since Lotus located in Dublin in 1984, more than 80 companies have followed its example. These include leading international names such as Microsoft, Oracle, Sun Microsystems, &-Com and Claris.

The computer industry is extremely diverse in both its products and activities. EDS and Andersen Consulting are involved in the development of large customised IT systems. IBM and ICL development teams in Dublin contribute to projects worldwide. Motorola, Ericsson and Isocor develop state of the art telecommunications software. Coerl produces graphics and multimedia products and Novell is a leader in networking software.

In addition to the large number of overseas operations, there are over 3,000 indigenous software companies servicing local and international markets from Ireland. These include sophisticated supply services such as localisation, disk duplication and technical support. There are also strong spin-offs to the printing industry. Clustering tends to produce these support and ancillary industries, often as spin-offs from the major players. This, in turn, increases competition and new businesses.

The potential and opportunities for the development and production of software are virtually unlimited. It is difficult to predict with certainty the likely increase in software jobs over the coming years. With the advance of the Internet, Dublin could become a content developer and publisher, having both the design and language skills necessary for European and US markets. Also Dublin has the potential to become a centre for excellence in the creation of content, in particular educational and cultural titles. This could form the basis of an educational services sector, especially with the necessity for lifelong learning in the rapidly changing information age.

Employment in the industry nationally is estimated to increase to 20,000 by the end of the century. However, there are already indications of personnel shortages in key areas. Adequate responses to this skills shortage need to be addressed immediately by the education and training authorities. In particular more people entering third level, and especially women, need to be encouraged into the technology sector.

Pharmaceuticals

The next wave of high value investment is hoped to come from the pharmaceutical and health care sectors and you will today find 10 of the top international medical products and 13 of the top international pharmaceutical corporations with branches here.

Financial Services

The mainly domestic banking, insurance and building society sector has seen employment growth of 15 percent over the last five years with the objective of creating a net 500 new jobs in this sector on an annual basis up to 2010.

The wider, global financial services sector (largely based in Dublin's International Financial Services Centre — IFSC — since its creation in 1987) has seen even more rapid jobs' growth, reaching 35 percent in 1996. It now employs over 3,500 people in more than 400 of the leading international financial concerns, handling an estimated US$100 billion of investment funds. These operations are leading to the growth of regional treasury, processing, support and service centres that themselves will soon employ nearly 2,000 people.

Financial services in Dublin employ some 30,000 people — a figure which has doubled in the last 20 years. Dublin houses the headquarters of Ireland's main banks, stockbrokers and insurance companies, as well as the rapidly growing IFSC. It has successfully combined the twin objectives of growing employment and economic activity while simultaneously contributing handsomely to the regeneration of a former docklands site.

With recovering strength in the worldwide financial services industry, and progress in the physical development of the site, the IFSC is becoming an international showcase for such projects. There are more than 500 approved for the centre, with over 370 already in operation, employing 2,500. Almost half are stand-alone projects, the remainder operating as agencies or captives. The strongest sectors are:

- Banking and asset financing
- Mutual fund management
- Treasury
- Insurance, including captive and reinsurance
- Securities trading

Total funds under management in 1996 amounted to £30 billion, more than double the December 1994 figure. Tax revenue now stands at £200 million, up from £142 million in 1995, and represents about 2 percent of total Corporation Tax Receipts.

Companies located in the IFSC can benefit from an incentive package that includes a 10 percent rate of corporation tax, relief from city rates, double rent allowance for tax purposes, and tax relief's for capital expenditure.

The original 1994 deadline for availing of the opportunity to establish in the IFSC has been extended to end December 2000.

Telecommunications

Business services have been the most rapidly expanding sector for new jobs in Ireland. These include retail, tourism and software, as well as other services such as telemarketing/call centres, distance learning, industrial services, and general services arising from increased manufacturing and growth.

Between 1992 and 1996, the number of people working in the business services sector of Dublin's economy grew by more than 72,000. The increase was more rapid in the 1990s when growth averaged almost 8,000 net new jobs each year.

The economy is growing at between 6–7 percent per annum, and the majority of services in this section are growing commensurately. In the past two years alone, over 20 major foreign companies have chosen Dublin as the base for their new European call centres. IDA-sourced multi-nationals with Dublin call centres include Best Western, Gateway 2000, Kao, Korean Air, Quartedeck International, UPS, Dell and Software Spectrum.

As technology progresses and develops, so too will its applications and uses. Home study (in addition to home banking and home shopping) will become a more prominent and effective means of education, particularly at third level. The utilisation of, and demand for, remote diagnostics (medical, engineering, and planning, etc) will increase rapidly, opening up huge possibilities/opportunities.

Internet

Telecom Internet (TI) may be a relatively new player in the Internet field, but it has set itself ambitious targets since it was set up late in

1997. TI wants Ireland to become the centre for all European Internet activity, much in the same way as Ireland has become a world capital for call centres. Many organisations with popular web sites are currently based in the United States, which can lead to congestion at peak times, so a possible solution would be to create mirror sites in Europe with Ireland bidding to be the lead site.

Tourism

Tourism is now one of the largest and fastest growing businesses in the country and the fastest growing indigenous-owned sector. Its contribution to GNP has grown from 5.4 percent in 1988, to 6.4 percent in 1995, and is set to exceed 6.5 percent for 1996. Forecasts suggest that it will become even more important than agriculture in under three years. The industry supported 107,000 jobs nationally in 1996, an increase of 39,000 since 1988. Since 1987, 30 percent of all jobs created have been supported by tourism and it now accounts for one in 12 of all jobs.

Construction of hotels (with over 25 at either planning stage or under completion) should generate considerable activity as the tourism sector continues to expand, and the international convention centre is expected to get underway in the next two years.

Overseas visitors to Ireland have doubled in the past decade. Last year tourist numbers grew by 10.7 percent and revenue by an estimated 12.5 percent. In 1996 4.7 million tourists visited Ireland spending £1.4 billion.

Irish tourism performance exceeds its European counterparts. Latest information from the World Tourism Organisation (WTO) confirms that Irish tourism growth, in terms of tourist arrivals, was double the world experience and almost treble the average European performance.

Tourism is now one of the highest growth areas in Dublin's economy, and an annual increase of 3,000 jobs in Dublin tourism from 1997 to 2010 is achievable. A combination of increased marketing, development of new tourism products and improvements to the fabric of the city, have made Dublin one of the fastest growing tourism destinations in Western Europe.

The results for 1995 and 1996 were highly encouraging for Dublin's tourism industry, showing continued growth in visitor numbers and revenue. The number of out-of-state visitors rose by 21 percent in 1995, and 16 percent in 1996, bringing the total number of visitors to over two and a half million — more than double the city's population. Tourism revenue also rose by 26 percent to £440 million in 1995, and to £475 million for 1996, including £105 million in hotels and guest houses, approximately £90 million in shops and around £150 million in pubs and restaurants.

Britain remains the biggest market (42 percent) for visitors to Dublin, with numbers up by 19 percent to 956,000 in 1995. Visitors from North America were also up by 26 percent to 83,000, with a lower growth from mainland Europe. The European market, however, is a particularly lucrative one, accounting for 39 percent of Dublin's tourist revenue.

Jobs in tourism do not appear in the official labour force classifications, and estimates for 'tourism supported jobs' must be used. Using this classification, the increase in the number of jobs generated by tourism in the Dublin region has been dramatic — rising from 14,000 jobs in 1986 to an estimated 29,000 jobs in 1996. The tourism industry is particularly important for Dublin since it is labour-intensive and can absorb numerous unskilled and semi-skilled workers, as well as professional workers in areas such as hotels, shops, restaurants and support services.

The Operational Programme for Tourism predicts an increase of 29,000 jobs in tourism in Ireland over the period 1994–1999, including development of the International Convention Centre which alone is estimated to support 1,500 jobs.

RETAIL

An average increase of 500 jobs per annum is achievable in the retail sector. Growth in retail sales and related employment was sluggish in the early part of the 1990s. The past two years have seen a stronger performance, with growth of about 6 percent in both 1995 and 1996. Around Dublin, new retail centres have come on stream in Blanchardstown and Jervis Street, to be followed by the Quarryvale and other developments. While these may involve some displacement of existing retail centres, continued growth in overall sales and employment is expected. The dominant trend in retail employment is towards part-time staff: this is expected to continue.

Once those major projects are completed, however, the scope for additional large-scale retail development in the Dublin region is likely to be more limited.

Construction Projects

Construction work on transport infrastructure will continue and large projects on the horizon include the tunnelled North Port Access Route, the Southern Cross and the LUAS light rail project.

Public Services and Utilities

Employment in public administration, including the defence forces, has been declining marginally in Dublin over the past ten years; the sector employs some 27,000 people, a decline of more than 4,000 in that time. This decline has resulted from government decentralisation programmes, and some reduction in overall employment in the non-commercial public service in the second half of the 1980s. Although there has been a rise in public service employment nationally in the first half of the 1990s, gains in the Dublin region have not been noticeable.

The pressure on government to reduce the overall public service pay bill, together with a likely continuation of decentralisation to areas outside Dublin, is likely to see the overall numbers employed in this sector in the Dublin region declining slowly over the next three to five years.

DOMESTIC AND INDIGENOUS INVESTMENT

Finally, it must not be forgotten that employment is being created by the Irish investing in their own future, creating small businesses to fill the many niches and opportunities that the expanding economy is generating. The numbers here are impressive with 130,000 new jobs coming from the small firm sector in the last three years alone, and with a predicted further 100,000 coming on stream by the year 2000.

The range of employment opportunities has thus widened as the investment from overseas has come pouring in, and new industries have been created. All of this has then led to the development of spin-off ancillary, supply and service jobs in tourism, construction, communications, retailing, the professions, health and medical care, the police, the security industry, education, etc. One more startling statistic is that more jobs have been created since 1993 than in the preceeding 30 years! The following table shows where these jobs have come from:

PRIVATE SECTOR EMPLOYMENT GROWTH 1990 TO 1996

Sector		Employment Growth	Percentage Growth
Manufacturing	Foreign	18,400	20%
	Indigenous	10,100	8%
International Services			
	Foreign	13,100	239%
	Domestic	3,800	69%
Other Services		120,000	30%
Other Industry		1,500	1%
TOTAL JOBS GROWTH		166,900	

The consequence of this growth is that by 1997 about 16 percent of the workforce was engaged in manufacturing (with 44 percent of these employed by overseas-owned companies) and 5 percent in financial services. The traditional industry of agriculture still accounts for some 13 percent of the workforce.

JOB HUNTING

One thing to bear in mind is that in Ireland private recruitment and placement agencies as well as the state run Jobcentres, are much more usual means of finding jobs than is direct advertising in the press — athough you should not neglect to scan the papers if you have the opportunity.

Should you be a United Kingdom citizen who has been registered as unemployed in the UK for at least four weeks, you should be able to continue to receive your Jobseeker's Allowance payment for up to three months, even while you actively seek employment elsewhere within the European Union. You will still have to sign on each fortnight, but you can do this at a recognised, local social security office, following which your welfare payment will be sent to you in local currency. As with many bureaucratic procedures, the rules are strictly drawn and enforced. You must complete the relevant paperwork — your UK Jobcentre should be able to provide you with this. In reality you may find this a difficult option to exercise.

MEDIA

The national papers to look out for include *The Irish Times Business Supplement* on a Friday, *The Irish Independent* on a Thursday and the Sunday papers, *The Sunday Independent* and the *Sunday Business Post*. Local papers will carry a range of job opportunities for their immediate area of circulation.

The Irish Times	http://www.irish-times.com
The Appointments Page	http://tap.gtc.ie/tap
Jobfinder	http://www.infolive.ie/jobfinder
Topjobs	http://www.topjobs.ie
The Irish Jobs Page	http://www.exp.ie
Computer Jobs	http://www.softskills.ie
and	http://www.corporateskills.com

AGENCIES

Recruitment Agencies make their money by charging the employer when a successful candidate is chosen, but are free for the candidates themselves — so make them work hard on your behalf. Choose the ones that specialise in your skills if you can, and keep in touch with them on a regular basis to ensure that they are fighting your corner.

A full list of employment agencies would be impossible to provide here, as there are so many, but you can find them listed by region in the various editions of Ireland's *Independent Directories*, their version of the UK's *Yellow Pages*.

Independent Directories Ltd
1-2 Upper Hatch Street
Dublin 2
Tel: (01) 475 2300
Fax: (01) 475 2301

FAS, LES AND JTS

One thing it seems you will soon have to get to grips with is the multiplicity of agencies, often known by their respective acronyms, that can help the unemployed person find work.

They are grouped together here as they are all state run and government financed and, in theory at least, should be able to guide you to the agency best suited to your needs, even if you initially approached the wrong one! It will be easier to sort through the programmes available in person once you are in the country and able to discuss your requirements and skills face-to-face with someone.

- FAS, which is the Irish for 'growth' has recently been combined with Forbairt, an agency aimed at promoting home-grown business, to form 'Enterprise Ireland'. It is the operator of local state training and employment offices and your local office is probably the most sensible starting point in your job hunt since these are the Jobcentres where you may wish to register as seeking employment. Also many employers advertise their vacancies there
- LES is the Local Employment Scheme, whose offices run various programmes
- JTS organises job-based training schemes through FAS and LES

There is a host of employment, training and work-place experience programmes in operation aimed at different social groups, each with their own particular hindrances to full-time employment. Many of these allow the candidate to continue receiving their welfare benefits, thus easing the transition from country to country.

HIGH SKILLS POOL AND EURES

These organisations are aimed at graduates and those with particular skills and qualifications. The intention is to keep them in touch with opportunities at home in Ireland even while they are overseas.

- FAS runs the High Skills Pool and organises a Jobs Fair each year in Dublin just after Christmas.
- EURES is run by the European Employment Service and aims to provide Irish people with information on employment openings across the European Union.

NETWORKING

One of the best sources of employment has traditionally been from personal contact, whether through relatives, friends and colleagues or directly through your own efforts. Unfortunately, this may not be much help to the new arrival who does not have a family base in the country and who has not built a web of contacts.

Employment Support Services
Department of Social Welfare
PO Box 3840
Dublin 2
Tel: (01) 704 3165

Irish National Organisation of the Unemployed
6 Gardiner Row
Dublin 1
Tel: (01) 878 8635

Local Employment Service
FAS
27-33 Upper Baggot Street
Dublin 4
Tel: (01) 668 5777

The High Skills Pool
Powerhouse
Pigeon House Harbour
Dublin 4
Tel: (01) 668 7155

STARTING A BUSINESS

Ireland's dynamic economic growth has been fuelled both by attracting large, international businesses and by encouraging small enterprises. As already explained, the Irish small business sector is thriving and now numbers about 160,000 enterprises this has created tens of thousands of jobs over the last few years and it is widely predicted that this boom will continue to create jobs for some time to come.

There exists a veritable plethora of agencies that are intended to help new firms to get started. They will provide advice on the various national and regional tax exemptions, reductions and holidays that are available, as well as giving help finding premises and employees, and on any training, grants and assistance packages. Bear in mind that few service sector enterprises qualify for state funding or support, though tourism is the principal exception to this rule. The central contact has to be:

Small Business and Services Division
Department of Enterprise, Trade and Employment
Davitt House
65A Adelaide Road
Dublin 2
Tel: (01) 661 4444

Small Business Support

The two agencies that you may well have contact with are part of Forfas — the Irish Development Agency (IDA) for incoming firms and Forbairt for indigenous businesses that have ten or more employees. Traditionally they have concentrated on manufacturing and exporting concerns. Both are located at:

Forfas
Wilton Park House
Wilton Place
Dublin 2
Tel: (01) 668 8444

Forfas produces a particularly valuable publication called *Innovation Ireland: A Directory of State Assistance for Industrial Innovation*. Other important state bodies include:

Udaras na Gaeltachta
Na Forbacha
Galway
Tel: (091) 503 100
Fax: (091) 503 101

Shannon Development
Town Centre
Shannon
County Clare
Tel; (061) 361 555
Fax: (061) 361 903

An Bord Trachtala Merrion Hall (The Irish Trade Board)
Sandymount
Dublin 4
Tel: (01) 269 5011
Fax: (01) 269 5820

An Bord Bia (The Irish Food Board)
Clanwilliam Court
Lower Mount Street
Dublin 2
Tel: (01) 668 5155
Fax: (01) 668 7521

Bord Failte (The Irish Tourist Board)
Baggot Street Bridge
Dublin 2
Tel; (01) 676 5871
Fax: (01) 676 4764

Bord Iascaigh Mhara (The Irish Fisheries and Fish-farming Board)
Crofton Road
Dun Laoghaire
County Dublin
Tel: (01) 284 1123

FAS (The Irish Training and Employment Authority)
27-33 Lower Baggot Street
Dublin 2
Tel: (01) 668 5777
Fax: (01) 668 3691

Micro Business Support

Aimed specifically at very small business, (those employing fewer than ten people), there are some 35 City and County Enterprise Boards that can provide advice and training, consultancy and study grants, and either employment or investment grants to both new and existing businesses. Being aimed at such small concerns, they will not usually countenance proposals requiring grants of more than £50,000 or total investments exceeding £100,000.

Area Partnership Companies

To bring even more assistance to particular areas of high and stubborn unemployment the Area Partnership Companies were specifically created. These companies have considerable local flexibility as to how they meet their local economic and employment challenges. They can be contacted via:

Area Development Management Ltd
Holbrook House
Holles Street
Dublin 2
Tel: (01) 661 3611
Fax: (01) 661 0411

Funding Your Business

In common with venture capital investors and lenders the world over, you will greatly enhance your chances of raising the necessary start-up funding if you can raise some of the required finance yourself. This shows personal commitment and the putting of your own money at risk is deemed to reinforce your drive for success.

The first approach for most people requiring smaller sums will be the banks and lending institutions, through arranging a loan or overdraft facility. Try not to give onerous personal guarantees, though in truth these are often insisted upon especially if you have no track record. The various institutions operate different funds that often tend to specialise in one particular type or size of enterprise, so shop around to find the most appropriate and understanding, as well as for the best deal as regards interest rates, guarantees and ongoing bank charges once you are up and running.

AIB Bank Enterprise Development Bureau
Bankcentre
Ballsbridge Dublin 4
Tel: (01) 660 0311
Fax: (01) 668 2009

Bank of Ireland Enterprise Support Unit
Head Office
Lower Baggot Street
Dublin 2
Tel: (01) 661 5933

Forbairt Fund operated by AIB, Bank of Ireland and Ulster Bank

ICC Bank
Head Office
72-74 Harcourt Street
Dublin 2
Tel: (01) 475 5700
Fax: (01) 671 7797

Irish League of Credit Unions
Lower Mount Street
Dublin 2
Tel: (01) 490 8911
Fax; (01) 490 4448

National Irish Bank
Head Office
7-8 Wilton Terrace
Dublin 2
Tel: (01) 678 5066
Fax: (01) 678 5949

TSB Bank
Head Office
114 Grafton Street
Dublin 2

Tel: (01) 679 8133
Fax: (01) 671 1239

Ulster Bank
Small Business Section
33 College Green
Dublin 2
Tel: (01) 677 7623
Fax: (01) 702 5875

Venture Capital

What is true of lenders as regards personal commitment is doubly true of venture capital companies, since they are buying a slice of your business. Remember that they are usually looking for a high rate of return and will have an eye as to how they can realise the growth in the value of their investment should it be successful, since it is capital value growth that constitutes their return on investment rather than merely securing their capital and charging an interest rate. Some of Ireland's more significant players in this field include:

ACT Venture Capital Ltd
Jefferson House
Eglinton Road
Donnybrook
Dublin 4
Tel: (01) 260 0966
Fax: (01) 260 0538

Bank of Ireland Entrepreneurs Fund
Head Office
Lower Baggot Street
Dublin 2
Tel: (01) 661 5933

Business Innovation Centres

These and the Dublin Seed Capital Fund operate the Investor Register Service to match investors with entrepreneurs as well as a capital fund.

Business Innovation Fund
Molyneux House
67-69 Bride Street
Dublin 8
Tel: (01) 475 3305
Fax: (01) 475 2044

Shannon Development
Town Centre
Shannon
County Clare
Tel: (061) 361 555
Fax: (061) 361 903

Smurfit Job Creation Enterprise Fund
94 St Stephen's Green
Dublin 2
Tel: (01) 478 4091
Fax: (01) 475 2362

Tax Relief for Investors

The Irish government has taken an active role in encouraging private individuals to invest share capital in unquoted companies, because it understands their value to the business community as awhole. The government has introduced a series of tax breaks whereby the sums invested — within certain carefully defined rules — can be offset against an investor's tax liability. The qualifying conditions, however, are complicated for all parties. You should certainly seek professional advice before embarking on such a scheme, and do so quickly: the current legislated reliefs expire on 5 April 1999.

Business Expansion Scheme
Direct Taxes Administration Branch
Office of the Revenue Commissioners
Dublin Castle
Dublin 2
Tel: (01) 679 2777 / Fax: (01) 671 0012

Compliance with Labour Laws

As an employer, even a small one, there are a number of laws that cover the conditions and safety of your employees that you will need to become familiar with.

The Department of Enterprise, Trade and Employment produces a very useful booklet which you should consult. Entitled *Guide to Labour Law*, it outlines concisely some of the many laws that you as an employer will come across and need to observe while operating in Ireland. These laws include:

- Contracts and Terms of Employment
- Wages and Minimum Rates in Certain Trades
- Working Time
- Notice Periods, Redundancy Schemes and Protection of Employment
- Registering as an Employment Agency
- Safeguarding of Employees' Rights
- Dismissals
- Employers' Insolvency Payments Scheme
- Children and Young Persons
- Safety, Health and Welfare at Work
- Worker Participation
- Industrial Relations

Registration

Do not forget to let the tax authorities know that you are setting up a business. In order to register your business for income and corporation taxes, value added tax and your status as an employer you will need either Form TR1 if you are a sole trader or part of a partnership, or TR2 for limited companies

The people to contact are:

The Revenue Commissioners
Employers' Information
Taxes Central Registration
9 Upper O'Connell Street
Dublin
Tel: (01) 874 6821

Further Sources of Advice and Assistance

As you can see from the details outlined in this chapter, it is not so much finding help with a new business that is difficult in the Republic, as much as finding the help that best meets your requirements! To point you in the right direction, here are some other useful contacts that could make a good starting point as seen from the 'user' end of the grant and assistance telescope rather than the 'provider'.

Forbairt

An Enterprise Link service provides a comprehensive source of information over the telephone. This will be able to advise you on the most appropriate agency for your purposes:

The Bolton Trust

This operates the Powerhouse and can offer space for rent and the services of an Enterprise Development Manager

Bolton Trust
The Powerhouse Pigeon House Harbour
Ringsend
Dublin 4
Tel: (01) 668 7155
Fax: (01) 668 7945

Business Incubation Centres

These primarily offer premises and facilities:

Richmond Business Campus
North Brunswick Street
Dublin 7

Ossory Business Park
Ossory Road
Dublin 3
Tel: (01) 807 2400
Fax: (01) 872 6252

Business Innovation Centres

There are six of these centres — Dublin, Cork, Galway, Limerick, Waterford and Derry. Their principal role is to provide a comprehensive business advice service principally for high tech and cutting-edge enterprises. Contact:

Business Innovation Centres
The Tower
IDA Enterprise Centre
Pearse Street
Dublin 2
Tel: (01) 671 3111
Fax: (01) 671 3330

Other Imporatnt Addresses

A source of start-up capital funding for small proposals, though you will need to find at least 50 percent of any requirement yourself:

First Step
Jefferson House
Eglinton Road
Donnybrook
Dublin 4
Tel: (01) 260 0988

If it is professional advice, planning, consultancy and feasibility studies that you need as well as help with formulating applications for grants and financial assistance then you could approach:

Liffey Trust
117-126 Upper Sheriff Street
Dublin 1
Tel: (01) 836 4651 / Fax; (01) 836 4818

National Microelectronics Application Centre
University College
Lee Maltings

Prospect Row
Cork
Tel: (021) 904092
Fax: (021) 270271

Project Development Centre
17 Herbert Street
Dublin 2
Tel: (01) 661 1910
Fax: (01) 661 1973

Useful Business and Professional Associations
Chambers of Commerce in Ireland
22 Merrion Square
Dublin 2
Tel: (01) 661 2888
Fax: (01) 661 2811

Irish Small and Medium Sized Enterprises Association (ISME)
32 Kildare Street
Dublin 2
Tel: (01) 662 2755

Irish Management Institute
Sandyford Road
Dublin 16
Tel: (01) 295 6911

Irish Business and Employers' Confederation (IBEC)
Small Firms Association (for businesses employing fewer than 50)
Confederation House
84/86 Lower Baggot Street
Dublin 2
Tel: 660 1011 / Fax: (01) 660 1717

Irish Congress of Trade Unions
19 Raglan Road
Ballsbridge

Dublin 4
Tel: (01) 668 0641
Fax: (01) 660 9027

Health and Safety Authority
Temple Court
Hogan Place
Grand Canal Street
Dublin 2
Tel: (01) 662 0417

CITIZENS' INFORMATION CENTRES
There are currently more than 80 of these centres providing free
and confidential advice on many topics affecting the person in the
street. They are registered with:

National Social Service Board
71 Lower Leeson Street
Dublin 2
Tel: (01) 661 6422 / Fax: (01) 676 4908

Association of Chartered Certified Accountants
9 Leeson Park
Dublin 6
Tel: (01) 491 0466

Institute of Chartered Accountants in Ireland
87 Pembroke Road
Dublin 4
Tel: (01) 668 0400

FURTHER READING
If all this seems too daunting for your initial approach then
*Enterprise Ireland: A Directory of Sources of Assistance for
Entrepreneurs and Small Business Owners* published by the Oak
Tree Press, could help. Oak Tree also publishes *Starting a Business
in Ireland*, which could provide you with some invaluable help
with the legal and administrative necessities.

CHAPTER 11

Education and Training

EDUCATION

The education of children is one of the most onerous duties for a parent since the choices made during these years will affect the whole of the child's life.

Fortunately Ireland has much to offer children, both from the academic, educational point of view as well as the opportunities for sport and leisure and being able to develop generally in a healthy and attractive environment.

Over many years in spite of, or perhaps because of, the lack of employment opportunities within Ireland itself, the Irish educational system has generally been considered to be of good quality and held in high esteem. Education is seen, quite literally, as a ticket out of the country into employment overseas. Ireland is now second only to Japan in the proportion of its young workers holding a scientific or engineering degree.

Although the domestic employment outlook has been transformed, the old values still apply and the government has invested heavily in the educational infrastructure at all levels. From regularly reviewing the curricula, increasing the number of selected, college-level course places by half, through to creating the opportunity for children to learn a second European language at primary school, the government has improved opportunities. Along with the emphasis on education there has been a similar commitment to skills, vocational training and adult learning.

Although the Catholic Church has traditionally held a considerable influence over the school system, and this is still often the case, the introduction of modern curricula and changing social attitudes mean that multi-denominational and co-educational schools are becoming much more popular as are the special *gaelscoileanna* where all teaching is undertaken in Gaelic.

The basic principles appertaining to each level of education and training will be described in greater detail, but here are some general points that will help build the framework:

- Almost two thirds of all four-year olds and nearly all five-year olds attend primary school
- Full time primary and secondary education is compulsory for children aged six to 16
- Some 86 percent of children currently stay on until aged 18, (known as Senior Cycle education). The government's stated aim is to push this figure to 90 percent by the year 2000. The costs of primary and secondary education are met by the government, though private schools do exist alongside the state system, but books and uniforms have to be paid for
- Certain tertiary level courses are also free of charge
- The curricula for both primary and secondary state schools are centrally set by the Department of Education, which is also responsible through a schools inspectorate for ensuring their implementation

You should consider whether you want to send your children to a school that is avowedly Catholic, centred on another faith, or multi-denominational in outlook; whether it is single sex or co-educational; whether the language of tuition is primarily English or Irish; and whether to go private or public.

Other important features to enquire about are common to all schools, such as the size and staff-to-pupil ratio, examination results, science, sporting, computer, language, music and library facilities available, or whether the school has any reputation in a particular subject area or for running especially good Transition Year Programmes (of which more later in the chapter).

PRIMARY OR FIRST LEVEL EDUCATION

The 3,300 primary schools spread among almost every town and village in the country accommodate about 98 percent of Ireland's half a million four to 14-year olds, with the balance attending one of the

115 special schools or 79 private, fee-paying ones. Such schools are commonly run by a board of management with a strong parental input, have around 25 pupils per teacher and tend to be fairly small with over half having fewer than four teachers.

The normal hours of attendance are between 9.30am and 2.00pm for the younger children, extended to 3.00pm for the older. Homework is set and there are, of course, the usual after-school sport and interest group activities.

All state-funded schools follow the national curriculum with private schools having greater flexibility, though in practice the need for pupils to gain the same qualifications leads to a commonality of courses.

SECOND LEVEL EDUCATION

Ireland's 370,000 students between the ages of around 13 and 18 attend one of four distinct types of school:

- Secondary/Fee-Paying: 61 percent of all students are in 452 private schools, most frequently run by a religious organisation.

- Vocational: 26 percent of all students are in 247 schools run by Vocational Education Committees that receive 93 percent of their funding from the state and provide free education.

- Community/Comprehensive: 13 percent of all students in 76 individually state funded schools also providing free education.

- International:a handful of schools that emphasise teaching in a foreign language to a foreign curriculum such as a French school in Dublin and a Japanese school in Kildare. In Dublin there is St. Killians where the Irish curriculum is delivered through English and German.

This second level education is divided into distinct cycles:

Junior Cycle

This is a three-year period to age 16 that leads to the Junior Certificate examinations at either Ordinary or Higher Level. Within this cycle students can — in theory — study as many topics as they like, but must study at least three subjects of the core curriculum (Irish, English, Mathematics and in some schools Religion) and at least four others from the national curriculum that includes such areas as History, Geography, Foreign Languages, Religion and Sciences. Other subjects such as Civics and Physical Education are not examination topics.

We say that students can 'in theory' study as many topics as they want: this is because a school will generally set its own core programme and may not be able to provide examination level teaching in every possible topic, some languages for instance where teachers may be in short supply.

Senior Cycle

This is where an optional Transition Year Programme is followed by a choice of three subjects that are studied for two years leading to a Leaving Certificate. The Transition Year Programme between achieving Junior Certificate and starting the Leaving Certificate, transition year courses have proved remarkably popular since there is considerable flexibility for teachers, parents, students and local businesses to contribute to the content in each school. The programmes typically include work experience, group and personal project work and vocational training.

The following table on page 140 may help summarise the above descriptive paragraphs of second level education.

To obtain a place at either a first or second level school you should apply to the individual school directly. For a list of appropriate schools in your area you can go through your local county, county borough, borough or urban district council. If you are new to an area that has a waiting list in operation you should make sure to apply for a place at the school of your choice at the earliest possible date.

THIRD LEVEL EDUCATION

Once the student has collected his/her leaving certificate there are a number of options open, from starting work, undertaking some form of vocational training, to continuing their education at a

CYCLE	OPTIONS	COURSE/SUBJECTS TAKEN
Junior	Compulsory	Irish, English, Maths and other subjects, higher or ordinary level. (3 years' duration)
Senior	Established Leaving Certificate	Irish, English, Maths plus 4 other subjects. Best 6 counted for third-level entry. (2 years' duration)
	Optional Additional Transition Year	Wide range of team and individual projects with creative, cultural or business theme. (1 year's duration)
Options	Leaving Certificate Vocational Programme	1 — Leaving Certificate subjects, 2 of which are selected from vocational subjects. 2 — 1 modern European language. 3 — 3 compulsory link modules, ie Enterprise Education/ Preparation for Work/ Work Experience. (2 years' duration)
	Leaving Certificate Applied	1 — General Education (minimum 30% of time). 2 — Vocational Education (minimum 30% of time). 3 — Vocational Preparation (minimum 25% of time). (2 years' duration)

DESCRIPTION	EXAMS/QUALIFICATIONS
Broad-ranging, structured programme. Students will take subjects in preparation for more specialised choices in senior cycle.	Junior Certificate: exams June, results September.
Very structured programme. Students may take any subject at higher or ordinary level. Leads to entry to third-level education.	Leaving Certificate exams in June. Results in August.
Very flexible developmental programme with extensive input into curriculum from students, parents, teachers, local business and community.	Depending on school, opportunity to gain extra-curricular qualifications.
Same as established Leaving Certificate, with concentration on technical subjects. Funded by European Social Fund due to vocational content. Leads to further vocational training, eg. PLC or RTC.	Leaving Cetificate
Self-contained programme for students who do not choose other Leaving Certificate options. Emphasis on person. Covers broad curriculum. Can leave to Post Leaving Certificate courses.	Applied Leaving Certificate.

higher level. If they choose the educational route, then they have the choice of going to a university college, a regional technical college, Dublin Institute of Technology or a college of education.

Admissions to all these institutions are handled centrally on a nationwide basis by the Central Applications Office that produces annually a complete listing of every course on offer from each college. Having discovered where the chosen topics are being offered the applicant can then obtain details from the relevant college.

Applications must normally be submitted with the appropriate fee by 1 February, but some late applications can be made up until 1 July. Places are then offered to the candidate during August, shortly after the Leaving Certificate results become available.

As stated earlier, the Irish set great store by a good education and the competition for places can be quite fierce, especially where a college has a strong reputation in a particularly popular specialism. To help with this you are able to apply for up to ten degree and ten certificate/diploma courses, so that at least something should come through!

Your chance of being offered the place at the top of your list depends on a points' system that is used both for grading the applicants and as an encouragement to study 'unpopular' but important subjects like mathematics. It is worth noting that you gain an extra 10 percent bonus for passing examinations in Irish.

LEAVING CERTIFICATE GRADE

% Range	Grade	Higher Paper	Ordinary Paper	Higher Maths
90-100	A1	100	60	140
85-89	A2	90	50	125
80-84	B1	85	45	115
75-79	B2	80	40	105
70-74	B3	75	35	95
65-69	C1	70	30	85
60-64	C2	65	25	75
55-59	C3	60	20	65
50-54	D1	55	15	
	D2	50	10	
	D3	45	5	

With the wide variety of institutions and courses available, there has been a need to produce 'modularised' courses which allow the student to progress through a course more-or-less at their own pace. This is especially useful for adults who are also in employment or who have family commitments. It also simplifies the process of re-takes, but does mean more examinations for full time students during their years at college. The other benefit is that a student can start with a lower level of certification and use this as a stepping stone up the qualification ladder. This can be especially useful if you failed to gain sufficient points on leaving school to enter your preferred course immediately.

Recognised Qualifications
National Certificate
A two-year course that leads to a technical qualification that tends to be vocational in nature.

National Diploma
An advanced version of the certificate requiring either an extra year's study after gaining a National Certificate or a three-year course in its own right.

Degree
Three or four-year courses leading to full, professional qualifications.

Private Colleges
There are private colleges, too, that offer a wide variety of courses, but check that they are 'bonded' in order to safeguard your fee (students at such colleges are not eligible for grants) and that the eventual qualification gained is a generally recognised one.

There are no fees for undergraduate courses in recognised third level colleges for Irish or European Union citizens who have been resident in Ireland or another European Union country for three of the five years immediately prior to making their application and who have not completed an undergraduate course anywhere else. Simply holding an Irish passport is not sufficient to qualify for a free college education.

COLLEGE TYPE	EXAMPLES
Universities	Dublin City University University College Dublin Trinity College Maynooth College
Inmstitutes of Education	DIT (7 colleges) College of Music, Waterford Institute of Education (status awarded 1997)
Regional Technical Colleges	Athlone, Carlow, Cork, Dundalk, Galway, Sligo, Letterkenny, Limerick
Colleges of Education	NCAD, Dublin, Crawford, Cork, Dun Laoghaire
Colleges of Art and Design	Open University Business School, Dublin
Open University	

DESCRIPTION	QUALIFICATIONS	STUDENT GRANTS
Top-tier third level. Primary post-graduate and research degrees	All universities award their own degrees	Yes, where students are eligible
Entry possible at all 3 levels of higher education	Degrees, diplomas, certificates	Yes
Specialises in engineering, science, construction, art and design	Mainly 2-year certificate courses, can lead to diplomas, degrees	Yes
Train primary school teachers	Degree in education	Yes
Dedicated exclusively to art and design	NCAD up to degree. Other certificates, diplomas	Yes
Distance learning with tutorial backup	Primary and higher degrees, professional qualifications	No, however tax relief on fees

Maintenance Grants are available through your local authority, but only on a means tested basis and provided that the candidate has been resident in Ireland for at least one year prior to applying. For further information contact the Department of Education at the address listed on the right.

ADULT EDUCATION

Educating and re-skilling the adult population is seen as vital to Ireland's further economic well-being and, as such, there have been considerable moves to make learning possible in this area and to encourage mature students to return to education.

The Vocational Training Opportunities Scheme operated by local Vocational Education Committees around the country offers programmes for lone parents and the unemployed, as well as being of particular help if you have been away from full time education for some time.

Dublin University runs a number of courses leading to a variety of qualifications including degrees on an outreach basis.

The Open University and the National Distance Learning Centre offer another route to gaining qualifications outside the traditional college based system.

The Department of Education produces a guide for mature students (those aged 23 or over) that gives details of full time Third Level courses available. Contact:

Adult Education Section
Department of Education
Hawkins House
Hawkins Street
Dublin 2
Tel: (01) 873 4700

LANGUAGES

Quite apart from the 70,000 teenage and 30,000 adult students who come to Ireland every year to learn English, there are opportunities to learn a foreign language for English speakers, too.

As well as the many language courses offered by various colleges, there are such organisations as Alliance Française, the Göthe

Institute, the Italian Cultural Institute, the Dutch Society and Gael Linn that have a variety of learning opportunities to offer interested students.

ACCREDITATION OF THIRD LEVEL COURSES

This is done by either a university or the National Council for Educational Awards. A course accredited by some other organisation should be considered with due care.

NON-IRISH QUALIFICATIONS

The European Community is working towards the interchangeability and mutual recognition of qualifications. However there is still a long way to go, given the multiplicity of school curricula, examination systems and higher level course lengths and contents that are currently in place across the member states. Given this, it is worth checking whether any of your qualifications are transportable to the Irish environment and whether you can gain any examination exemptions or need to gain some transitional qualification before embarking on a particular course of study at an Irish institution. Useful addresses are:

Department of Education
Marborough Street
Dublin 1
Tel: (01) 873 4700

National Parents' Council
16-20 Cumberland Street
South Dublin 2
Tel: (01) 678 9981
For Primary Schools

National Parents' Council
Marino Institute of Education
Griffith Avenue
Dublin 7
Tel: (01) 857 0522
Post Primary Schools

Central Applications Office
Tower House
Eglinton Street
Galway
Tel: (091) 63318

AONTAS
National Association of Adult Education
22 Earlsford Terrace
Dublin 2
Tel: (01) 475 4121

National Council for Educational Awards
26 Mountjoy Square
Dublin 1
Tel: (01) 855 6526

Universities
Apply to the respective Admissions Office

University College
Cork
Tel: (021) 276871

University College
Belfield
Dublin 4
Tel: (01) 706 7777

Dublin City University
Glesnevin
Dublin 9
Tel: (01) 704 5000

University College
Galway
Tel: (091) 524411

University of Limerick
Limerick
Tel: (061) 333644

St. Patrick's College
Maynooth
County Kildare
Tel: (01) 628 5222

Trinity College
Dublin 2
Tel: (01) 677 2941

Regional Technical Colleges
Athlone Regional Technical College
Athlone
County Westmeath
Tel: (0902) 24400

Carlow Regional Technical College
Carlow
County Carlow
Tel: (0503) 70400

Cork Regional Technical College
Cork
County Cork
Tel: (021) 545222

Dundalk Regional Technical College
Dundalk
County Louth
Tel: (042) 34785

Galway Regional Technical College
Galway
County Galway
Tel: (091) 753161

Letterkenny Regional Technical College
Letterkenny
County Donegal
Tel: (074) 24888

Limerick Regional Technical College
Limerick
County Limerick
Tel: (061) 327 688

Sligo Regional Technical College
Sligo
County Sligo
Tel: (071) 43261

Tallaght Regional Technical College
Dublin 24
Tel: (01) 404 2000

Tralee Regional Technical College
Tralee
County Kerry
Tel: (066) 24666

Dun Laoghaire College of Art and Design
Dun Laoghaire
County Dublin
Tel: (01) 280 1138

Dublin Institute of Technology
Dublin
Tel: (01) 402 3000

Waterford Institute of Technology
Waterford County
Waterford
Tel: (051) 302000

VOCATIONAL EDUCATION

Since every county has at least one institute that delivers courses under the umbrella of its local Vocational Education Committee there are too many to list individually. However, if you require further information on them in a given location you should either contact the appropriate county authority or approach the national body:

The Vocational Education Association
McCann House
99 Marlborough Road
Dublin 4
Tel: (01) 496 6033

TRAINING

As well as the education of its children and young people, the Irish government is very keen to up-skill and re-train its workforce to enable people to meet the challenge of the higher quality jobs that are being actively and successfully attracted into the country by the various development initiatives.

Such training is also seen as a key element in the numerous programmes to encourage the unemployed and lone parents back into the workforce and out of total reliance on the benefits and welfare infrastructure, as well as to equip those who left school with few or no qualifications with the ability to find better quality employment. The government recently brought out a White Paper on Human Resource Development, a far reaching document on the mechanics of just exactly how to fulfil the potential for development of people after they leave the formal education ladder.

The three key elements are:

- To encourage employers and employees to recognise and pursue the importance of investing in people
- To put in place an innovative training infrastructure capable of meeting ever changing skills requirements
- To have positive support for those who find it difficult to maintain themselves in the world of work

COLLEGE TYPE	EXAMPLES	DESCRIPTION
Certificate	Locations nationwide	Tourism
Agricultural Colleges	Co-ordinated by Teagasc	1-year courses with practical element
Nursing	17 general and 6 specialised hospitals, all linked to third-level college or university	3 years
Apprenticeships	FAS nationwide	2-3 years, 7 phases of training
Private colleges	Options nationwide	Variety of courses including degree
Distance education	Oscail, the National Distance Learning Centre	Wide range of degrees and post-graduate courses

QUALIFICATIONS	STUDENT GRANTS
Certified in Ireland and the EU	Weekly allowance, books, uniform
Certificates can lead to RTCs	Allowances
Diploma from associated college	Grant for uniform, books
International crafts certificate	Allowance
Depends on certification	Generally no, some tax relief for courses over 2 years
Degrees, post-graduate qualifications, professional qualifications	No

The range of available programmes is quite extensive and is constantly evolving, so you should contact:

National Employment Service
FAS
27-33 Upper Baggot Street
Dublin 4
Tel: (01) 668 5777

As an independent subsidiary of FAS the National Employment Service is responsible for the development of national level placement and guidance services and administering various positive action programmes such as Community Employment, Jobstart, the Back to Work Allowance Scheme, VTOS and Job Clubs as well as developing the Local Employment Scheme network.

REGISTERING WITH A GENERAL PRACTITIONER AND DENTIST

When you move into a new area it is highly advisable to find yourself a general practitioner (GP) and a dentist to cover the normal run of medical problems, especially if you take part in sport, have small children, are elderly or are suffering from a chronic disorder of some sort. There are a number of ways of finding a GP and a dentist, the best way being by word of mouth — a personal recommendation of good service is always worth following up — but failing that, scan through the local Golden Page directory or make enquiries of the Regional Health Board for a selection of practitioners in your area.

CHAPTER 12

Health Care

Health care is increasingly important to people and with growing prosperity comes ever increasing demand for health services. Ireland is no exception to this rule and aims to provide a comprehensive health care service available to all. As the delivery of health services is expensive, and the demand apparently unlimited as technology and science advance, the Irish long ago decided to build an essentially insurance-funded system. As a result, a quite extraordinarily high percentage of the population have some level of private cover through one of the two providers described a little later.

As a tourist or visitor you should ensure that you have adequate and appropriate medical emergency insurance cover in order to pay for any hospital or medical bills and perhaps to get you home. You will have to pay the bills first and then make a claim on your insurer afterwards. Citizens of European Union member states can benefit from the mutual agreements that exist between the countries concerned. For instance, a United Kingdom citizen should carry a Form E111 that will entitle the bearer to be seen free of charge at a hospital as well as by a general practitioner or dentist registered with the relevant Regional Health Board.

If you are living in Ireland then, in order to be entitled to use the Irish public health services, you must normally be ordinarily resident in the country or belong to one of the categories of persons covered by European Union legislation.

If you meet one of these criteria and are entitled to use the service there is yet another division. You will have either:

- Category 1 Eligibility, which entitles you to the full range of services for free

- Category 2 Eligibility, in which case you are only entitled to a limited range of services

To qualify for fully free health care you have to pass a means test in order to receive a Medical Card from one of the eight Regional Health Boards that administer the public health service in Ireland. The income levels vary according to certain criteria, ranging between around £90 and £150 gross weekly income, but earning below the relevant bench mark will entitle you to free care that includes:

- Treatment by a general practitioner
- Prescriptions
- Full in-patient hospital care in public wards
- Full out-patient public hospital services
- Dental, ophthalmic and aural services and appliances
- Maternity and infant care services

As an elderly person in receipt of certain social security pensions from a European Union member state you, too, could qualify for a Medical Card and hence free healthcare services regardless of income. This is provided though that you do not also receive an Irish social welfare pension and are not in employment or self-employed.

Without a Medical Card you will have to pay for such services as:

- Being seen by a General Practitioner (typically £20 per visit)
- Prescriptions and medicines
- Dental, ophthalmic and aural services and appliances

All rules regarding health care entitlement tend to become hideously complicated and there can be benefits available to people who meet the following conditions:

- Aged under 21   39 weeks PRSI paid since first starting work
- Aged 21 to 24   39 weeks PRSI paid since first starting work and 39 weeks PRSI paid or credited in relevant tax year of which minimum 13 weeks must be paid contributions

- Aged 25 to 65   260 weeks PRSI paid since first starting work and 39 weeks PRSI paid or credited in the relevant tax year of which a minimum of 13 weeks must be paid contributions
- Aged over 65   260 weeks PRSI paid since first starting work and 39 weeks PRSI paid or credited in either the last 2 tax years before reaching 66 of which a minimum of 13 weeks must be paid contributions

The Ordinarily Resident Category 2 person — ie some one who does not qualify for a Medical Card — has to pay for the health care services listed above but is entitled to receive the following:

- Full in-patient hospital services in public wards, subject to a £20 per day charge for accommodation to a maximum £200 in any 12-month, consecutive period
- Full out-patient services
- Attendance at Accident and Emergency (Trauma) departments, though there is a charge of £12 for self- referrals, but none if referred by a physician
- Maternity and infant care services up to six weeks after giving birth

As a citizen of a European Union member state, you can qualify for a Medical Card under special EU rules and would not be subject to the standard means testing, though you would have to provide details of your income to establish the validity of your claim under these special rules. If you receive an Irish social welfare pension or are employed or self-employed in Ireland, then the EU rules do not apply and you would have to satisfy the means test regulations to qualify.

People aged between 16 and 25, including students, who are financially dependent on their parents, would only be entitled to a Medical Card if their parents are already Medical Card holders, too. There are schemes to alleviate the cost of long-term medicinal requirements. Your general practitioner or pharmacist should be able to advise you on your eligibility.

ELDERLY PATIENTS

For elderly people in particular the Health Boards can provide or organise the following services, either directly or in combination with local voluntary organisations. Their availability can vary widely from region to region — and may not be available at all — and you should check whether there are any charges that will be made:

- Public health nursing
- Home help and meals on wheels
- Day care services
- Day centres and clubs
- Physiotherapy
- Chiropody
- Laundry service
- Various hospital services (such as medical assessment and rehabilitation)
- Respite care for carers and dependent elderly people (contact the National Rehabilitation Board in Clyde Road for full details)

State-run and private residential and nursing homes, including those specifically for the elderly, are inspected and ranked by the Department of Health and Children. But, as is often the case, demand tends to exceed supply, which puts a premium on finding a place. Of course the relative costs have a strong bearing on the demand: the cost of private homes can be alarmingly high. There is a rigorously assessed means-tested Nursing Homes Subvention, or subsidy, available, that must be applied for before entering the home. In order to qualify you must be 'sufficiently dependent and unable to pay any or part of the cost of maintenance in the home'.

There are three levels of financial support depending on whether you are assessed as having medium, high or maximum dependency. The means test will take into account not just your assets — the imputed value and income of any assets of yourself and your spouse or co-habiting partner, though the family home can be exempted under certain conditions — but also the ability to contribute financially of any children aged over 21. These are tough conditions and advice should be sought well in advance if it looks as though you may need to apply for this particular help.

PRIVATE HEALTH INSURANCE

Ireland has just two private health insurance providers, namely the Voluntary Health Insurance Board (VHIB) and the familiar BUPA.

The VHIB is a governmen-founded, non-profit-making organisation dating from 1957. It now has 1,400,000 members. It was given a monopoly of private health insurance until European Union legislation forced an opening of the Irish market in 1994, which led to BUPA's entry into the market in 1996.

One important feature of the Irish market is the notion of 'Community Rating', which essentially means that all adults (people over 18) pay the same premium for the same cover irrespective of age or perceived risk. The positive feature of such a system is that elderly people, especially, benefit from affordable premiums at a time when their usage of health care services is increasing. This is in marked contrast to risk-based pricing that tends to price out the elderly.

Within the 'Community Rating' system there are different levels of cover and service on offer, so you still have to shop around and find the package best suited to your particular requirements. Remember to read the contract rules and conditions and the small print very carefully!

To highlight a few features:

- VHIB covers 102 hospitals, BUPA 74
- BUPA will provide 100 percent hospital cost cover, VHIB varies between 92 percent and 97 percent
- Both cover out-patient services
- BUPA will pay towards home births and some homeopathic treatments
- VHIB adult premium applies from age 18, BUPA's from 21 if still in full-time education
- Both operate group plans with discounted premiums
- Both VHIB and BUPA premiums are eligible for tax relief at 26 percent

If you currently have private health insurance you may well be able to transfer directly into an Irish scheme, so contact your insurer directly for information on this.

UK NATIONAL HEALTH SERVICE

Your entitlement to free health care under the UK National Health Service will normally end once you cease to be resident in the UK.

If you have a current health condition that requires specialist care, treatment or monitoring, such as heart, cancer or that for children then you should contact your relevant Regional Health Board as to the availability of facilities in that area.

EMERGENCY SERVICE NUMBER

Finally, remember that the Emergency Service Number in the Republic is the same as in Britain — 999.

USEFUL CONTACTS AND ADDRESSES

Department of Health and Children
Hawkins Street
Dublin 2
Tel: (01) 671 4711

Eastern Health Board
Health Board Headquarters
Dr Stevens' Hospital
Dublin 8
Tel: (01) 670 0700
For Dublin, Kildare, Wicklow

Midland Health Board
Arden Road
Tullamore
County Offaly
Tel: (0506) 21868
For Offaly, Westmeath, Laois, Longford

North-Eastern Health Board
Navan Road
Kells
County Meath
Tel: (046) 40341
For Louth, Cavan, Meath, Monaghan

Mid-Western Health Board
Catherine Street
Limerick
Tel: (061) 316 655
For Limerick, Clare, Tipperary North

North-Western Health Board
Manorhamilton
County Leitrim
Tel: (046) 55123
For Donegal, Leitrim, Sligo

South-Eastern Health Board
Lacken
Dublin Road
County Kilkenny
Tel: (056) 51702
For Kilkenny, Carlow, Waterford, Tipperary South, Wexford

Southern Health Board
Cork Farm Centre
Dennehy's Cross
County Cork
Tel: (021) 545 011
For Cork, Kerry

Western Health Board
Merlin Park Regional Hospital
Galway
Tel: (091) 751 131
For Galway, Roscommon, Mayo

Directory of Social Service Organisations
National Social Services Board, 7th Floor, Hume House
Pembroke Road
Ballsbridge
Dublin 4
Tel: (01) 605 9000

Retirement Planning Council of Ireland
27-29 Pembroke Street Lower
Dublin 2
Tel: (01) 661 3139
Fax: (01) 661 1368

Voluntary Health Insurance Board
VHI House
Lower Abbey Street
Dublin 1
Tel: (01) 872 4499
Fax: (01) 799 4091

BUPA
12 Fitzwilliam Square
Dublin 2
Tel: (01) 662 7662

Irish Society of Chartered Physiotherapists
Royal College of Surgeons
St Stephens Green
Dublin 2
Tel: (01) 402 2148

Irish Society of Homeopaths
Prospect House
Newcastle
County Wicklow
Tel: (01) 281 0030

The Homeopathic Association of Ireland
66
92 Connolly Street
Nenagh
County Tipperary
Tel: (067) 34677

Disability Resource Centre, National Rehabilitation Board
44 North Great Georges Street
Dublin 1
Tel: (01) 874 7503

National Rehabilitation Board
25 Clyde Road
Dublin 4
Tel: (01) 668 4181

Irish Wheelchair Association
Aras Chuchulainn
Blackheath Drive
Clontarf
Dublin 3
Tel: (01) 833 8241

National Council for the Blind
P.V. Doyle House
45 Whitworth Road
Drumcondra
Dublin 9
Tel: (01) 830 7033

Catholic Institute for the Deaf
40 Drumcondra Road Lower
Dublin 9
Tel: (01) 830 0522

Alzheimer Association of Ireland
St John of God Hospital
Stillorgan
Tel: (01) 288 1282

Asthma Society of Ireland
15 Eden Quay
Dublin 1
Tel: (01) 878 8511

CHAPTER 13

Civil Rights and Duties

This is a very heterogeneous chapter that sweeps up a number of outstanding matters that do not fit naturally within any of the others, a fact that is in no way intended to underestimate or demean their significance and importance. Far from being unimportant, in fact, some of these items could mean the difference between a new and happy life and utter disaster.

Your local Citizens Information Centre is a good starting point for advice on your specific situation with regard to any of the following areas should you feel that they apply to you. Check for your nearest centre in your local *Golden Pages* telephone directory or, as they are centrally registered, you could approach:

The National Social Service Board
71 Lower Leeson Street
Dublin 2
Tel: (01) 661 6422
Fax: (01) 676 4908

VOTING

Every citizen should exercise their right to vote for the people that govern them. An old-fashioned view, perhaps, and one that those of us brought up under relatively free and democratic systems tend to take for granted and often simply ignore utterly, taking no active part in our governance at all except to grumble about it.

Voting in Ireland

So, lecture over, down to the mechanics of voting in Ireland. The key date for the putative voter is their 18th birthday, because — provided, on the year of the election, you are aged over 18 by 15 February and legally resident on 1 September — then you are entitled to register for the purposes of voting. Ireland, like most modern democracies, has a collection of bodies over which the electorate can exercise their mandate, namely:

- The European Parliament
- Ireland's National Parliament — the Dail
- County
- County borough
- Borough
- Urban district council

These are the most significant. As to which of these bodies you are actually entitled to vote for, you have to determine your particular class of citizenship:

- Irish citizens — can vote in all elections and referenda
- United Kingdom citizens — can vote in Dail, European and local elections
- Other European Union citizens — can vote in European and local elections
- Non-European Union citizens — can only vote in local elections

Unlike the United Kingdom, referenda form an important element of the Irish constitution and its democratic process. Recent referenda have been on such socially important matters as divorce and abortion.

Voting in the United Kingdom

If you have moved from the United Kingdom you may want to maintain your right to vote in UK General and European Elections. This can be done provided you fulfil all of the conditions outlined in one of the following groups:

Group 1

- You are a United Kingdom citizen
- You have been entered on the Electoral Register in the past

- You were living in the United Kingdom on the qualifying date (10 October in England, Scotland and Wales and 15 September in Northern Ireland.)
- That the period of time between the qualifying date when you were last entered on an Electoral Register and the one for which you are now applying does not exceed 20 years

Group 2

- You are a United Kingdom citizen
- The date of the qualifying day for the register on which you are applying to be entered is less than 20 years since you last lived in the United Kingdom
- You were below the legal voting age on the qualifying date immediately before you left the United Kingdom
- You had a parent or legal guardian entered on the Electoral Register at the address at which you lived when under the voting age in the above condition
- You are old enough to be legally registered to vote (currently 18, which age you must reach before the register on which you wish to be entered comes into force, being the next 16 February after the qualifying date)

In either case you will note that you cannot select where to register, but are tied to the address, and therefore the constituency, at which you were last deemed eligible to vote.

Each electoral register only remains in force for a year, so you will have to continue to re-register annually. To do this, complete an Overseas Elector's Declaration (Form RPF 37) which you can get from your local consulate or embassy. Once your registration has been approved, you will be sent a new form each subsequent year. As either of the above listed sets of conditions is quite tough and must be complied with in full, you will need to be able to prove that you meet them by having on hand the relevant documentation.

Voting by Proxy

The actual voting process is done by appointing a proxy, not by exercising a postal ballot. The proxy casts your vote on your behalf under your instruction. They, too, must pass certain conditions:

- They must be a citizen of the United Kingdom, the Republic of Ireland or a Commonwealth country
- They must be a United Kingdom resident
- They must be legally able and willing to act as a proxy

The paperwork for appointing your proxy is included in your Overseas Elector's Declaration form.

JURY SERVICE

Connected with your right as a citizen to participate in elections is your duty to participate in the judicial process as a juror. In Ireland, every citizen aged between 18 and 70, who is registered to vote in Dail elections, is liable for jury service under regulations set out in the Jury Act, 1976.

SEPARATION AND DIVORCE

With its strong adherence to the Catholic Church, the Irish have long held major objections to divorce, holding to the letter of the marriage ceremony that states that only death of a partner can end the sacred rite of marriage.

But times change, and Ireland has introduced civil divorce through the Family Law Act, 1996 that came into force on 27 February 1997. Once the civil divorce decree is granted, either party of the now dissolved marriage is free to remarry regardless of the grounds on which the divorce was sought, but both parties remain guardians of any children that may have been born during wedlock.

Separation can be regarded as a kind of halfway house: the parties remain legally joined, even though they choose to lead their own lives. In Ireland this is covered by the Judicial Separation Act, 1989 which provides for either party to apply to a court for the granting of a decree of judicial separation.

If you are already a divorced person, then check that your divorce is legally recognised in Ireland. It may not be if it was authorised by an institution not recognised by the Republic, and this could dramatically effect your decision to make a new life in Ireland.

Contacts on the subjects of marriage and divorce include:

Accord
All Hallows College
Dublin 9
Tel: (01) 837 5649
For marriage counselling

Aim Family Services
6 D'Olier Street
Dublin 2
Tel: (01) 670 8363 / Fax (01) 670 8365
For non-directive counselling, legal advice and family mediation

Parental Equality
54 Middle Abbey Street
Dublin 1
Tel: (01) 873 0108
Support group for people undertaking joint custody and shared parenting

Family Mediation Service
Block 1, Floor 5
Irish Life Centre
Lower Abbey Street
Dublin 1
Tel: (01) 872 8277
Fax: (01) 878 7497
Mediation service for separating couples

Catholic Marriage Counselling Service
39 Harcourt Street
Dublin 2
Tel: (01) 478 0866

DOMESTIC VIOLENCE

No doubt domestic violence has been around for as long as we have been a species that valued the nuclear family unit. However, we now regard such behaviour as utterly reprehensible. In Ireland the Domestic Violence Act, 1996 provides for the legal welfare, safety and protection of married and co-habiting couples, parents, children and others that live together in a domestic relationship. These safeguards are enforced through the issuing of Safety Orders, Barring Orders and Protection Orders.

Women's Aid
PO Box 791
Dublin 1
Tel: (01) 874 5303 / Fax: (01) 874 5525

HOMOSEXUALITY

The legality of homosexual relationships is another recent area of reform. Homosexual relationships are now much more readily accepted than in years past — in fact Dublin now plays host to an annual Lesbian and Gay Film Festival in the late summer. Homosexuality was decriminalised by the introduction of the Criminal Law (Sexual Offence) Act, 1993. The legal age of consent for homosexuals is 17, the same, incidentally, as it is for heterosexual relationships.

DISCRIMINATION

Ireland has very recently passed two laws, the intention of which is to root out a whole range of discriminations. The Employment Equality Act, 1997 concerns matters arising at the workplace and the Equal Status Act, 1997 relates to education, the provision of personal property and services, accommodation and registered clubs. Both acts cover the issues of gender, marital and family status, sexual orientation, religion, age, disability, race, colour, nationality, national and ethnic origin and membership of the travelling community.

CONSUMER RIGHTS

The individual consumer in Ireland has the right to expect certain minimum standards when renting or purchasing goods and availing themselves of services that are intended for private use. These standards are enshrined in the Sale of Goods and Supply of Services Act, 1980. Similar transactions undertaken in pursuance of a business, trade or profession or received by way of a gift may well not be covered by this legislation. It is with the private person that we are concerned here and in broad terms you should expect goods to be of 'merchantable quality', 'fit for their purpose' and 'as described'. You should also expect that services will be delivered by someone with the necessary skill, who will exercise proper care and diligence and use materials and goods that are sound and of merchantable quality in their own right. These legal rights cannot be diminished by any special clauses, but can be and often are exceeded by a supplier.

If you feel you require redress, you should first approach the supplier or retailer. If this fails to give satisfaction, you could next approach a third party, such as the relevant trade association or the manufacturer. Ultimately you have the right to go to law as a last resort, perhaps trying the Small Claims Procedure in the local District Court if your claim does not exceed £600.

Office of the Director of Consumer Affairs
4-5 Harcourt Road
Dublin 2
Tel: (01) 402 5555
Fax: (01) 402 5501

European Consumer Information Centre
13A Upper O'Connell Street
Dublin 1
Tel: (01) 809 0600
Fax: (01) 809 0601

European Consumer Information Centre
89-90 South Mall
Cork
Tel: (021) 274099
Fax: (021) 274109

Consumers' Association of Ireland
45 Upper Mount Street
Dublin 2
Tel: (01) 661 2466

LEGAL AID

The Legal Aid Board operates a number of law centres where you can apply for civil legal aid and advice. This is means tested, and to be eligible you must have a disposable income (after paying tax and rent) of £7,350 per annum. Even then you will usually have to make some contribution. If your income is a social welfare payment (such as an old age pension) you will have to pay at least £4 for advice and £23 for legal aid.

Legal Aid Board
St Stephen's Green House
Earlsfort Terrace
Dublin 2
Tel: (01) 661 5811

Free Legal Advice Centres
49 South William Street
Dublin 2:
Telephone: (01) 679 4239

Criminal Legal Aid can be obtained by application to the Court where you are appearing.

BIRTHS, DEATHS AND MARRIAGES

It is a requirement that these milestones be recorded for officialdom. Remember that children born in Ireland are regarded as Irish. If you want dual nationality or a foreign nationality to be recorded on the birth of a child, you should check with the authorities of the country concerned, as regulations vary widely from state to state.

Registrar General's Office
Joyce House
8-11 Lombard Street East
Dublin 2
Tel: (01) 671 1000
Fax: (01) 671 1243

CHAPTER 14

Living in Ireland

Once you are based in Ireland, building your life at the workplace or social gathering, there are a number of things with which you will need a degree of familiarity in order to survive. In the first section of this chapter we set forth some of the most ubiquitous institutions that you will find it hard to avoid.

BANKING

The banking system is very similar to the British with four big associated banks that operate a clearing system for other institutions. The Bank of Ireland, AIB, National Irish Bank and the Ulster Bank dominate the market, followed by a number of other banks such as the Trustee Savings Bank, ACC Bank, ICC Bank and the Irish Permanent Bank.

To open an Irish bank account you will need two forms of identification and proof of address, thereafter the normal rules apply regarding overdrafts, loans and interest. But, importantly, local managers retain the autonomy to grant loans and overdraft facilities to a much greater extent than is now the current practice in the United Kingdom.

All banks will have the facility to transfer funds between Great Britain and the Republic, but check with the bank concerned regarding any particular restrictions, taxes or charges that may affect your personal position, especially if moving money outside the European Community.

Being a highly competitive field, you should shop around for the best charging structure for your particular service requirements. For example, if you are aged over 55 you may be entitled to make some foreign exchange transactions without paying commission.

Bank Opening Hours

Typically, these are similar to elsewhere — 9.30am to 4.00pm Monday to Friday, sometimes with a late opening until 5.00pm on one day a week.

ACC Bank
ACC House
Upper Hatch Street
Dublin 2
Tel: (01) 478 0644
With some 49 branches

AIB Bank
Headquarters
Bankcentre
Ballsbridge
Dublin 4
Tel: (01) 660 0311
With some 327 branches

Bank of Ireland
Head Office
Lower Baggot Street
Dublin 2
Tel: (01) 661 5933
With some 300 branches

ICC Bank
32 Harcourt Street
Dublin 2
Tel: (01) 475 5700
With some 5 branches

Irish Permanent Bank
56-59 St Stephen's Green
Dublin 2
Tel: (01) 661 5577
With some 91 branches

National Irish Bank
7-8 Wilton Terrace
Dublin 2
Tel: (01) 678 5066
With some 60 branches

Trustee Savings Bank
Frederick House
South Frederick Street
Dublin 2
Tel: (01) 679 0444
With some 80 branches

Ulster Bank
33 College Green
Dublin 2
Tel: (01) 677 7623
With some 114 branches

BUILDING SOCIETIES

Traditional building societies are the property of their members, but
— as in the United Kingdom — there are moves to change them
into public companies and more bank-like businesses, using wind-
fall lump sum payments to the members as an inducement. The Irish
Permanent became a bank in 1994 and ICS Building Society is
owned by the Bank of Ireland. It is expected that First National
Building Society will turn itself into a public company soon.

Building Society Opening Hours

Typically 9.30am to 5.30pm Monday to Friday, sometimes with a late
opening until 7.00 or 8.00pm on at least one day a week and often
Saturday mornings, too

Educational Building Society
30 Westmoreland Street
Dublin 2
Tel: (01) 677 5599
With some 50 branches

First National Building Society
Skehan House
Booterstown
Dublin
Tel: (01) 283 1801
With some 77 branches

ICS Building Society
Haddington Centre
Percy Place
Dublin 2
Tel: (01) 611 3000
With some 7 branches

Norwich Irish Building Society
33-35 Nassau Street
Dublin 2
Tel: (01) 671 7181
With some 10 branches

CREDIT UNIONS

Credit Unions were created to help small investors and borrowers on a co-operative, not for profit, community level. They have become quite popular and have spread across the country, offering competitive rates on savings as well as insurance and health schemes and lending small sums to their members at very good rates. There are over 700 branches in existence with varying opening hours and facilities and you can find out about your local ones by contacting their representative organisation:

Irish League of Credit Unions
33-41 Lower Mount Street
Dublin 2
Tel: (01) 490 8911
Fax: (01) 490 4448

TELEVISION AND RADIO

The fledgling Republic of Ireland was quick to recognise the impor-

tance of a national broadcasting service and in 1926 Radio Eireann
was founded. This has remained the flagship radio service of Radio
Telefis Eireann, the state-sponsored broadcasting corporation, since
those times. Now known as RTE Radio One, the service provides the
full range of news, music, drama, features, current affairs, education,
religious, agricultural and sports programming. In 1972 this single
channel was joined by Raidio Na Gaeltachta to provide an exclu-
sively Irish language service, and in 1979 by 2FM, the pop music
channel. FM3 is the newest service and caters to those who prefer
their music to be classical. There is also a more regional service,
Radio Cork, based in Ireland's second city — the Irish are very sen-
sitive to the problem of the country becoming dominated by a
Dublin-centred culture.

Alongside these national stations you will often be able to
receive other worldwide broadcasts on FM, AM and Long Wave (BBC
Radio channels are within broadcast range of wide swathes of
Ireland) so there is no shortage of choice for either the casual or dis-
cerning listener.

In 1961 RTE commenced television broadcasting, firstly with
RTE 1 which remains the principal channel providing the range of
scheduling choice that you would expect to see these days including programmes from home-grown Irish production units, popular
British and American imports, chat and quiz shows, sports, news and
documentaries, etc.

In 1978 Network 2 was launched to provide a similar foil to
RTE 1, as BBC 2 is to BBC 1, or Channel 4 to ITV in Britain. Most
recently, in 1996, Teilifis Na Gaeilge was brought to the small screen
to provide a service for the Irish language speaking community. It
is remarkably successful, and regularly attracts the viewing of
280,000 adults a night, which is about 8 percent of the adult Irish
TV audience.

In many areas of Ireland you can also receive BBC 1 and BBC 2
(without paying the licence fee!) and some of the ITV stations.
Satellite channels are receivable with the appropriate equipment
and a growing network of cable television services are becoming
available

To watch RTE television broadcasting legally you will need to
buy an annual television licence, currently costing £75.

TELECOMMUNICATIONS — TELECOM EIERANN

Like the Post Office, Telecom Eierann is a state-owned body and has expanded to become a very modern and forward thinking business. There are also two other service providers to corporate customers, TCL and Esat Telecom.

Because of its inward investment and economic planning, Ireland has become a major player in the telecommunications industry with a large number of major companies basing their telecentre operations there. If you are in the United Kingdom and telephone Gateway Computers in London, or if you are in Germany and telephone Avis Cars, then your call will be answered in Ireland, though the response will be in the language of the country of origin of the call.

The latest telecommunications technology is available to every household and business and Telecom Eierann is the first company to install a complete small town with internet facilities to study the use and effect of 'Web Life' in a rural community, the guinea-pig being Ennis in County Clare and its 17,000 inhabitants.

Example Charges from Ordinary Phones
These include VAT at 21 percent:

Standard Rate:	From 8.00am to 6.00pm Monday to Friday
Reduced Rate:	From 6.00pm to 8.00am Monday to Friday, all day Saturday, Sunday and Public Holidays
Weekend Trunk Rate:	From midnight on Friday to midnight on Sunday and all day on Public Holidays
Calls to Mobiles:	Standard Rate for calls to mobiles applies from 8.00am to 8.00pm Monday to Friday
Reduced Rate calls to mobiles:	From 8.00pm to 8.00am Monday to Friday and all day Saturday, Sunday and Public Holidays

TELEPHONE CHARGES IN THE REPUBLIC OF IRELAND*

LOCAL

Direct Dial	Operator-Assisted
Standard Rate: 11.5p per 3min	Standard Rate: 72p for the first 3min or part thereof (minimum) and 11.5p per each subsequent 3min or part thereof
Reduced Rate: 11.5p per 15min or part thereof	Reduced Rate: 72p for the first15min (minimum) and 11.5p per each subsequent 15min or part thereof

TRUNK

	Direct Dial			Operator-Assisted			
	Standard Rate	Reduced Rate	Weekend Rate	Standard Rate		Reduced Rate	
	Amount of time per 11.5p Unit			First 3 min	Each extra min	First 3min	Each extra min
A Rate: to 56km	66.7sec	100sec	10min	£1.0	13p	86p	8.5p
B Rate: 56+km	31.7sec	47.6sec	10min	£1.40	27p	£1.11	17p
Calls to Mobiles	25sec	37.5sec	37.5sec	£1.80	40p	£1.40	27p

As in Great Britain the use of mobile phones has greatly increased. In Ireland mobile phone use has increased threefold over recent years bringing mobile phone use to 9 percent of the population and is likely to grow as quality, reliability and coverage increase. But check that your service provider will provide coverage in Ireland before travelling there intending to use yours!

POST — AN POST

The state owned An Post is the only recognised nationwide organisation for postal deliveries. It is modern and efficient (with only the occasional trade dispute) and operates a national and international service. In Dublin and one or two smaller cities, there is a selection of courier businesses, but they usually only supply a local, limited or premium-priced service.

Postage Costs

- The cost of a letter is 30p anywhere within Ireland (there is no first and second class post)
- It costs 30p to send a letter from Ireland to the United Kingdom
- It costs 32p to send a letter from Ireland to mainland Europe

The service aims to deliver within Ireland by the following day, to the UK in 1 or 2 days and Europe in 2 or 3

The network of Post Offices is very comprehensive and is thus used as a conduit for paying bills, distributing welfare payments, the selling of various licences, etc, as well as offering a variety of savings schemes and money transfer facilities.

CHAPTER 15

Leisure

The pursuit of happiness is regarded in some circles as a fundamental human right, and if the availability of opportunities to pursue sport and leisure activities is any measure, then the Irish are in pursuit of happiness big-time!

The range of choice is very great, from the outdoor and physical to the indoor and intellectual. If you have a particular hobby or obsession then it could be important to you to choose a home that is conveniently situated geographically speaking to facilitate your chosen interest. From the grand Georgian houses of Dublin, to the hustle and bustle of Cork, and on to the wide open spaces of Donegal, Ireland has a lot to offer.

While this book is certainly not intended to be a guide for the tourist — there are dedicated books aplenty on the delights of Ireland for the holiday maker — it does no harm to whet your appetite a little. If you require more information then the local tourist information office or the Irish *Golden Pages* (their version of *Yellow Pages)* can be very helpful.

First, one has to mention the uniquely Irish sports of hurling and Gaelic football. Both traditional games, their modern forms stem from the 1880s with the founding of the Gaelic Athletic Association by Michael Cusack (James Joyce's 'The Citizen' in his masterwork *Ulysses*) with the aim of reviving, codifying and protecting these very particular Irish sports as well as encouraging the Irish Gaelic language. The overtly political and nationalist purpose of their revived origins should not be forgotten, but today they are simply sports to be played, watched and supported like any other. The sporting highlight for both occurs in September, when they hold their respective All-Ireland final in Dublin's Croke Park stadium.

HURLING

As with many things Irish, the provenance of hurling stretches back to the mists and myths of pre-Christian Celtic Ireland. It is played all over the country by 15 players on each side, who attempt to score goals by hitting a hard ball the size of a cricket ball through their opponent's goal posts. To do so they use hurleys, sticks similar to those used in hockey. The goal posts are 20ft high and 20ft apart (6m high and 6m apart) with a crossbar set 10ft (3m) up; a ball passed under the bar scores three points and passed over just one. After two 30-minute halves the team with the highest points score wins. There are no stops for minor injuries!

GAELIC FOOTBALL

Not as old as hurling, Gaelic football's pedigree reaches back to medieval times when entire villages or parishes engaged in what can only be described as a melée rather than a game. It lasted all day and was fought across country. The game today retains its fluidity and can seem something of a free for all when first seen, but this is misleading and you soon appreciate the skill and relentless activity that require dedication, discipline and practice.

ROAD BOWLING

A curious, and even quirky, little sport still played on the public highway in parts of Cork, Waterford and Limerick. Two players compete against each other by rolling a 16 to 28 ounce (c.450-800gm) iron ball called a 'bullet' over a set distance in the minimum number of throws, with penalties for ending up off the road. Technically illegal for blocking traffic, the Garde turn a blind eye, though for how long this will remain the case is hard to judge.

HORSE RACING

One has to mention the particular Irish bonding with horses. In Celtic mythology and rites, the horse was especially prized as the most sacred of all animals, valuable for sport, as well as training for war. 2,000 years on, the Irish still worship the horse as evidenced at one extreme by the working-class Dublin children who keep them in their urban environment, through — at the other — to the number of fine race-courses, world class bloodstock breeders, trainers and jockeys and internationally important races on the flat and over the sticks (steeplechasing). In fact, it is said that the Irish invented steeplechasing when in 1752 two Cork gentlemen named Blake and O'Callaghan raced for 4.5 miles (7km) across country between two church steeples jumping any obstacles found en route.

Between the devoted horse keeper and the big money horse industry comes the great mass of people who simply love the atmosphere and excitement of a race meeting. Whether you are serious, career gamblers or pick-with-a-pin punters, it is great fun to chat with other race-goers and discuss the finer points of horseflesh — even ignorance is no problem after a few stouts!

The spirit of the ancient horse fairs can be found alive and well with annual events such as the Laytown Strand Races held every summer on a beach 30 miles (48 km) north of Dublin, the Killarney Summer Meet, Galway Races and the Great October Horse Fair at Ballinasloe in the east of County Galway, supposedly the market where Napoleon's famous mount Marengo was purchased. More traditional racing is carried on at a number of tracks, the best known being

- The Curragh, southwest of Dublin, the centre of County Kildare's horse industry with most races held between March and November. With the Irish National Stud is situated nearby, the Curragh is the centre if Irish horse racing and its major flat races are the major races of the Irish season and play an important part in British, if not world, horse racing:
  Irish 1,000 Guineas in May
  Irish 2,000 Guineas in May,
  Irish Derby in June
  Irish Oaks in July
  Irish St.Leger in September
- Leopardstown, a few miles south of Dublin, is another important home of flat racing as well as being a major course for National Hunt racing (over the jumps.)
- Punchestown holds one of the most fashionable events in April
- Fairyhouse hosts the Irish Grand National on Easter Monday
- Navan, Gowran, Galway and are other important National Hunt courses.

- Smaller tracks are situated in Ballinrobe, Bellewstown, Dundalk, Clonmel, Downpatrick, Down Royal, Kilbeggan, Limerick, Mallow, Roscommom, Sligo, Thurles, Tipperary and Wexford with fun, holiday meetings at Killarney, Tramore, Laytown, Tralee and Lostowel.

For the serious horse trader and breeder there is the Dublin Horse Show, held every August in the salubrious environs of the Dublin suburb of Ballsbridge. *The Irish Field, Sporting Life* and Irish Tourist Board's *Calendar of Events* all publish dates of meetings and form guides.

HUNTING

Hunting is quite popular, with as many as 85 recognised packs in existence in recent times, mostly of foxhounds. The season runs from October to March and it is often possible to hire a horse and join in if you are so inclined. The Irish Tourist Board or local riding centre should be able to provide details.

EQUESTRIANISM

Throughout the country there is a wide choice of riding facilities that cater to every rider, novice or experienced, young or old. Whether trekking and riding across heath and farmland, along mountain and forest trails or along miles of empty, sandy beaches there will surely be something for you.

GREYHOUND RACING

Not as popular as the ponies, but with its own atmosphere and dedicated following, there are 18 top class tracks in Ireland including Shelbourne Park and Harold's Cross in Dublin. For more information contact:

Bord na gCon (Irish Greyhound Racing Board)
104 Henry Street
Limerick
Tel: (061) 316788
Fax: (061) 316739

FOOTBALL (SOCCER)

The Irish Football Association regulates soccer in Ireland. Though popular, it lags behind the Gaelic sports and is still largely amateur, hence the consternation expressed recently over the rumoured arrival of the large, professional and, by Irish standards, wealthy Wimbledon FC. Ireland does produce many world class footballers who are often to be found in English and Scottish clubs and we have all been captivated by the spectacle of the Irish team's successes on the international arena in recent years under Sir Jackie Charlton's management.

RUGBY UNION

Landsdowne Road is the home of Irish rugby and rugby holds a special place in most Irish hearts. The Irish will tell you that they invented the game because William Webb Ellis was born in Ireland and exported the handling game to Rugby School — or so the story goes!

Ireland's first rugby club was formed at Trinity College, Dublin, in 1854 with the first game in 1855. The game spread and there were soon regular matches between colleges and senior schools, until on 14 December 1874 the Irish Football Union was established.

Ireland played their first international against England at the Oval in London on 15 February 1875 and they lost. Unfortunately Ireland's international record has been somewhat bleak, but they have had some success with their first Triple Crown achieved in the 1893/94 season. In the 1920's and 1930's they won the Championship once and had a share in the title four more times. Since then Irish successes have been few and far between, but they still manage to produce excellent players who are regular names in the British Lions summer tours and they always get a passionate following whether in Dublin or abroad.

Whether win or lose Irish players are always ready to smile, joke and share a pint. With the introduction of Italy to create a Six Nations Championship and the decision to accept professionalism into the sport, the Irish will be as hard as ever to beat and will come out onto the field to huge cheers for the emerald green. There are 250 clubs throughout the country with 12,000 adults and 34,000 juniors, so in almost every town and city you will never have far to look to join or support your local team.

CRICKET

Not a lot of cricket gets played in Ireland as historically it was seen as an 'English' sport and was therefore shunned by nationalist Irish patriots; indeed the Gaelic Athletic Association when founded banned its members from playing any non-Gaelic games at all.

Despite this unpromising beginning the Irish national team is to be seen playing in various international tournaments and will always be remembered for having beaten the great West Indies in a 1969 one-day game after having skittled them out for only 25.

TENNIS

Tennis courts are to found all over Ireland, with the usual mixture of grass and clay, indoor and outdoor, public or municipal and private club.

ANGLING

Ireland, with its 9,000 miles of fishable rivers, over 1.5 million hectares of lakes and 2,000 miles of coastline, offers superb opportunities for all manner of anglers, be they coarse, game, sea, boat or match fishermen and women of whatever level of experience. There is a wide variety of fish to be caught, and some of the most scenic locations anywhere in Europe.

The only thing to remember is that waterways may well be state or privately owned, so permission should be sought. For salmon and sea trout (not brown or rainbow trout) fishing you will need a licence and there is special conservancy legislation covering the fishing of pike.

The country is divided into areas under Regional Fisheries Boards who will advise on fishing areas, legislation and issue salmon and sea trout licences. A variety of licences are are available:

All districts, full season, adult	IR£25
All districts, full season, juvenile	IR£8
Single district, full season	IR£12
Twenty-one days (tourist)	IR£10
One day (tourist)	IR£3

As regards other species, Ireland is divided into eight fisheries development areas, the purpose of which is to conserve and promote fish stocks. In both the Northern and Shannon Fisheries Development Areas you will need to obtain a share certificate, whereas in the other areas the purchase of certificates is voluntary.

Annual	IR£12
Twenty-one days	IR£5
Three days	IR£3

The best advice an give is to consult the Bord Failte for advice and information before setting out.

WATERSPORTS

Also making use of Ireland's abundant coastal and inland waters, Atlantic swells and plentiful windpower are a wide variety of divers, waterskiers, paragliders, surfers, windsurfers, sailors, canoeists and general lovers of all kinds of being under, in, on or even over water.

As you would expect, certain areas favour certain activities and have special facilities, so check with your travel agent or the Bord Failte for specific information on your favoured sport.

GOLF

Golf has seen explosive growth in popularity over recent years with many international standard courses being developed. A combination of an all-year grass growing season and the tourist bonanza have all fuelled the transformation of this sport into a major industry; not forgetting the, perhaps surprising, passion with which the Irish themselves have taken to the game given their tradition of more physical and contact oriented sports.

As you would expect, there are courses that cater to all levels of player and depths of pocket, from the exclusive, member only clubs to the relaxed and friendly places where you can turn up with your clubs and play a round for a modest fee.

Golfers from around the world come to Ireland to enjoy the variety of locations. Over 260 courses, open links, clifftop and lakeside, many hosting international tournaments beckon the golfer from the first to the 19th hole!

THEATRES AND CONCERT HALLS

Throughout time Ireland has enjoyed a rich association with the arts and for such a small country has produced a disproportionate number of world renowned poets, actors, writers, musical ensembles and latterly film producers and dancers (*Riverdance*, etc). This heritage is set to continue to flourish especially with the tax concessions that the government has used in recent times to encourage the arts in general and film making in particular.

Most large towns possess at least one theatre, such as Cork, Galway, Limerick and Dublin and these produce the full range of theatrical events embracing pantomime, Broadway and Westend shows, modern and classical. There are several annual festivals, many of long standing; The Galway Arts Festival in July, the Kilkenny Arts Week in August and the Dublin Theatre Festival in October.

As mentioned in an earlier chapter, music has always been part of the Irish cultural scene and Ireland has produced many fine composers such as Seoirse Bodley, Brian Boydell, Shaun Davey, Turlough O'Carolan, A J Potter, Sean O Riada and Michael Suilleabhain.

Classical works are catered for by the National Symphony Orchestra of Ireland that plays at the magnificently restored National Concert Hall in Dublin. Telephone Dublin (01) 475 1572 for forthcoming event information.

Traditional Irish music — the music of Uillean pipes, bodhrán, harp and fiddle — is very actively promoted by the Comhaltas Ceoltoiri Eireann organisation through 400 or more branches spread across the globe to wherever the Irish reached.

CINEMAS

The cinema is as popular in Ireland as elsewhere and, again, most large towns will have at least one showing the usual mixture of films to attract all tastes. In fact Ireland often gets to see major Hollywood blockbusters before they are premiered in Britain! Increasingly, too, the beauties of Ireland have tempted film makers.

HOUSES AND GARDENS

Mention 'house' in the Irish context and you are likely to visualise an image of solid, stone-built, turf-roofed cottages set amidst expanses of green countryside and surrounded by a potato patch.

How wrong can stereotypes be? Ireland has some truly magnificent grand, stately homes dotted across the land often dating from the 18th century and the height of the English ascendancy. Indeed, the Georgian buildings of Dublin are as fine as any to be seen in the British Isles. As well as other stately homes there are numerous public gardens, including the fascinating Botanical Gardens at Glasnevin, Dublin, home to a fine collection of many thousands of specimen trees, shrubs, flowers and plants of all kinds from every habitat on the earth.

Powerscourt Estate, just 12 miles south of Dublin City, is an area known as 'The Garden of Ireland', being a collection of gardens within a garden covering a thousand acres of beautifully planted styles — a Japanese garden, an Italian garden and the longest herbaceous border in Ireland!

SHOPPING

The law of numbers has a huge impact on shopping everywhere and Ireland is no exception. In the cities and surrounding areas you will find the greatest variety, whether it be furnishings, clothing, white and brown goods. All major brands are available, often alongside a similar, local equivalent manufactured by an Irish company.

With food and groceries you will again find the full range of products available, but you will also find a very good selection of salads and vegetables (many organic) along with superb ranges of Irish cheeses and dairy products, pies and sausages, cakes and biscuits and you will find that most regions have their own speciality foods.

You will, however, find it harder to exotic ingredients, but things are improving and the selection is increasing along with the many coffee bars, but again mainly in the larger urban centres.

PUBS

There is nothing quite like a traditional Irish pub for an introduction to Irish life. This is the place where you will experience the 'craic', come across a Gaelic poetry and music recital, stumble into a wake or wedding party (you may not always be sure which it is!)

Pubs come in all shapes and sizes; the pub that is one half bar and one half grocer; the pub no bigger than the average, cottage living room — actually is somebody's living room! The great Victorian or Edwardian gin-palace; the quiet wood-panelled haunt of serious drinkers and dedicated smokers.

Some pubs are famous for their unique architecture or interiors, others for their antiquity ('The Brazen Head' in Dublin traces its history back to 1198) and many for simply being good pubs where the barman 'pulls a good pint'.

The pub is the centre of social life where you cannot fail but to soak up the atmosphere and will soon be planning your itinerary and agenda to justify your next visit and another pint and a chat. The attractions of the Irish pub have made it such a success that there are now more than 1,350 Irish pubs around the world making it possible to order your stout and Irish stew from Shanghai to San Francisco. Much copied, but never bettered, the best place to find an Irish pub has still to be Ireland.

RESTAURANTS

When you think of Irish food what springs to mind first is Irish smoked salmon, Irish stew, soda bread and the ubiquitous potato. But add to that list Galway oysters, black sole, Howth crab, Wexford mussels and fields of fresh, organic vegetables and herbs. Mix with Italian olive oil, Thai spices and Pacific rim flair and innovation and you create a fusion of style and taste that takes Irish produce to new heights never previously scaled. Irish cooking, like so much else, has gone through a dramatic change in recent years and this mélange of Irish foods and global flavours can be experienced in some fine restaurants throughout the country.

It is common for restaurants to be licensed to serve wine only, not draught beers or stouts, but the wine lists are often comprehensive, selecting the best from around the world. Outside the main urban centres restaurants are quite restrictive in their hours of opening; with lunch between 12.00 midday–2.00pm and dinner 7.00–9.00pm, so it pays to check before setting out and if possible to book.

CAFÉS ETC

Quality coffee bars and cafés can be found throughout — Bewley's in Dublin being the most famous, offering the usual assortments of light meals, snacks, cakes and pastries at reasonable prices. A popular development is for the larger book shops to house such places. Pubs will often provide good, wholesome, simple food all day long, but not evenings as this 'interferes with serious drinking!' and on Sundays often serve a traditional Sunday roast which attracts much enjoyed by family groups.

Fast food has arrived and can be found everywhere; burgers, pizzas, fish and chips, kebabs, fried chicken and the rest all having their place in the modern Irish eating pantheon.

Conclusion

So there we are, a quick run around the block covering the delights and dangers, pleasures and pitfalls of moving to Ireland. If nothing else we would hope to have whetted your curiosity and given you a desire to visit the country — even if just for a vacation. If you are considering buying property or finding employment then we would hope to have provoked not only some serious planning and forethought, but also provided some answers and useful avenues for further exploration along with a list of names and addresses of useful organisations.

Above all, to make your move a success you must enter into the spirit of Ireland as the Spirit of Ireland embraces you.

Notes